s

ast

A guide to t… …ure reserves in coastal Suffolk

Written by Jenny James
Production Team: John Grant and Malcolm Key
RSPB Editorial Advisor: Ian Barthorpe

This guide has been part-funded by the following organisations

Suffolk Coast & Heaths
Area of Outstanding Natural Beauty

R.H.AMAR & CO. LTD. Famous for Fine Foods

Ufford Park WOODBRIDGE HOTEL·GOLF·SPA
Gateway to Suffolk's Heritage Coast...

The Grimwade Charitable Trust

RSPB

ISBN No. 978-0-9563162-4-0

Published by the
Woodbridge Local Group of the Royal Society for the Protection of Birds,
Riverside, Parham, Woodbridge, Suffolk, IP13 9LZ.

Printed by
Healeys Printers Ltd, Unit 10-11, The Sterling Complex,
Farthing Road, Ipswich, Suffolk, IP1 5AP

Front cover main photograph: Avocet, by AMANDA HAYES
Back cover photograph: Minsmere, by ANDY HAY (rspb-images.com)

The Suffolk Coast

Part of the Suffolk Coast & Heaths Area of Outstanding Natural Beauty, showing the RSPB reserves featured and their access roads

CONTENTS

FOREWORD

by Mike Clarke

RSPB Chief Executive

A lot has happened in the 80 years since the RSPB's first presence on the Suffolk coast. When we employed watchers to keep an eye on the stone-curlews nesting at North Warren in 1932, few people could have anticipated the significance of this area, not just as one of the best areas for watching wildlife in the UK, but for the many conservation success stories that can now be told.

One of the most famous stories is the return of the avocet to the UK. Absent as a breeding bird for more than 100 years, these elegant wading birds arrived from the near- Continent in the spring of 1947. The RSPB swung into action and established nature reserves at both Minsmere and Havergate Island to protect these new arrivals.

The rest, as they say, is history. Avocets are now widespread in many parts of the UK, and their return is celebrated in the choice of this lovely bird to adorn the RSPB logo.

The RSPB now manages more than 2,000 hectares along the Suffolk coast, stretching from Dingle Marshes in the north to Hollesley Marshes in the south. These nature reserves are home to an incredible variety of wildlife, from the tiniest insects to mighty oak trees.

Minsmere may be famous for its nesting avocets, bitterns and marsh harriers, but it is also home to a greater biodiversity than any other RSPB nature reserve. This is testament to the careful management of the varied habitats and detailed monitoring by RSPB staff and volunteers.

The RSPB has already stepped up for nature by providing the perfect conditions for many species to thrive. Through our Suffolk Coast Futurescape initiative we are working with many landowners and conservation partners in the area to step up for the wildlife of the wider countryside, helping declining species such as yellowhammers, bumblebees and bluebells. Such work is only possible thanks to the continued support of individuals, through their membership subscriptions, donations and entry fees.

As a visitor, you may be unlikely to see many of the smaller, rarer or more elusive species, but whenever you visit our Suffolk coast nature reserves you can be sure of a great day out. The recently expanded visitor facilities at Minsmere, for example, offer something for everyone: café, family activities, birdwatching hides and gorgeous countryside walks.

You'll find an incredible variety of wildlife at our nature reserves too. The reedbeds at Dingle Marshes, Minsmere and North Warren are home to otters, water voles, rare moths and, of course, bitterns. On the heathland at Minsmere, North Warren and Snape, you'll find Dartford warblers, adders and grayling butterflies.

Huge flocks of ducks and geese visit the grazing marshes at Minsmere, North Warren and Boyton Marshes every winter, while Havergate Island is home to a thriving population of brown hares.

This book celebrates all of these stories and more and is the perfect introduction to the wildlife and history of this magnificent stretch of coastline. I congratulate the RSPB Woodbridge Local Group for their hard work in compiling such an excellent guide. I hope you enjoy reading it and exploring the area.

M J Clarke

MIKE CLARKE

RSPB

ACKNOWLEDGEMENTS

This is an updated and expanded version of *Spread Your Wings*. It keeps the structure and format of the original publication without which our task would have been considerably more difficult. It is therefore with great pleasure that I acknowledge the skill and dedication of Dr Jenny James, biologist (author), and John Grant, journalist (book designer), along with Philip Dodd at Healeys, the printers, who were also part of the original team and have therefore contributed to both the first and second editions of this publication. In addition, Sarah Ricks, at Healeys, has provided invaluable publishing support for John Grant.

The Suffolk coast and its RSPB reserves in the area are dynamic, with new reserves being added to the RSPB portfolio of sites, such as the new Snape Reserve, and mature reserves, such as Minsmere, being constantly modified and improved for wildlife and people. Climate change is likely to exacerbate the dynamic nature of these habitats, making it more difficult to write the definitive guide to these outstanding reserves. To give some direction to these possible changes, Paul Forecast, RSPB Regional Director, has written a new section to help us assess and quantify the impact of these changes.

Since the first edition of this book in 2004, new species of birds and wildlife have spread to many of these reserves – and some species, unfortunately, have been lost. This book attempts to catalogue these changes. The detailed reserve information documented in this book has been obtained from the RSPB reserve wardens, without whose knowledge and expertise this guide would not have been possible. Special thanks go, therefore, to Mel Kemp at Minsmere, Dingle Marshes and Dunwich Forest, David Thurlow at North Warren, David Fairhust at Snape, Aaron Howe and Kieren Alexander at Havergate, honorary wardens Reg Etheridge and Dudley Sheppard at Boyton Marshes and Hollesley Marshes respectively, and Alan Miller of the Suffolk Wildlife Trust – Site Manager of Dingle Marshes. Ian Barthorpe, RSPB Marketing & Publicity Officer, has been the fourth member of the project team. He has given considerable advice throughout and exercised RSPB editorial control. Rob Macklin was Area Manager until 2011 and much of the knowledge and enthusiasm for these Suffolk coastal reserves came from him.

A comprehensive range of photographs has been assembled for this publication from many individuals and organisations, many of whom have provided their services free of charge. Particular mention must be made of Jon Evans' superb bird pictures and Mike Page's aerial photographs. All photographers have been credited where their photographs have been used.

Sponsorship is the lifeblood for small charitable projects and this one has only been possible because five organisations have chosen to support this RSPB Woodbridge Local Group initiative, but special mention must be made of the Suffolk Coast & Heaths Unit's generous contribution to the printing costs.

We are fortunate indeed to have these wonderful places on our doorstep, but protecting and developing them in a sustainable way will need the constant dedication of the RSPB and its professional support team. We thank Mike Clarke, RSPB Chief Executive, for fully endorsing this project and writing the Foreword for this publication.

M. Key.

MALCOLM KEY

Project Co-ordinator, RSPB Woodbridge Local Group

The Only Constant in Conservation is Change

by Paul Forecast
RSPB Regional Director, Eastern England

Nature reserves are among the most tangible ways in which the RSPB delivers nature conservation. Thanks to the ongoing support of our members and other supporters we are able to manage these wildlife gems in perpetuity, thereby providing a permanent home for wildlife.

When you visit the RSPB nature reserves on the Suffolk coast you could be forgiven for thinking that this permanence means that landscape is static and unchanging or that 'nature reserves' are left for nature to dictate the rate of change. But you couldn't be more wrong.

All habitats on the Suffolk coast are going through constant change which is indiscernible to the eye, but if left unchecked each habitat would become oak woodland. Ungrazed heaths and grasslands are quickly colonised by scrub species such as gorse and silver birch which build up sufficient nutrients in the soil to allow oaks to follow. Wetlands silt up allowing fen plants to colonise. As a mat of fen vegetation becomes established it creates enough soil structure to allow trees that like damp conditions, such as alder and willow, to grow. Over time they dry out the wetland soil, allowing silver birch and then oaks to become established.

In order to maintain the variety of species that you see on the Suffolk coast our wardening staff and volunteers spend their time looking to arrest this change to provide a variety of habitats which in turn support the needs of different species of birds, mammals, insects, plants and other wildlife. It should be noted that we want some oak woodlands too!

The challenge of maintaining a mosaic of habitats is well understood and we are well practised in the management of the natural processes that we are looking to control. However, there is a new change that we are only just beginning to understand which, if not managed properly, could result in the loss of the habitats and species that make the Suffolk coast unique and this is – climate change.

How will climate change affect the wildlife on the Suffolk coast?

Climate change is predicted to have widespread and potentially damaging impacts on nature. We are already seeing the signs of climate change in Suffolk with drier summers, stormier winters, signs of spring coming earlier and the onset of autumn arriving later. What does this all mean?

Out of sync...

Wildlife has a life cycle that changes with the seasons and with particular dependencies at certain times of the year – for example, blue tits feed their nestlings when there are plenty of caterpillars. Climate change is already bringing spring forward. Flowers such as snowdrops and bluebells are coming into bloom earlier, oaks are leafing earlier and butterflies are appearing on the wing earlier. There is considerable evidence, and growing concern, that climate change will increasingly stretch, and potentially break, the seasonal links that have evolved between species. Birds may be forced to nest at different times in response to the changing availability of the food they depend on to feed to their young.

Too much water, too little water...
We are experiencing wetter springs which could result in birds such as waders which nest on the ground, for example at Boyton Marshes reserve, having their nests flooded. Drier summers could make it much harder for them to find insect-rich wet pools to feed on. At Minsmere it is increasingly difficult to find enough freshwater to keep the Scrape wet for migrant waders which need soft mud in which to feed.

If sea levels rise saltwater will inundate and erode the saltmarshes at places such as Boyton Marshes and threaten the river walls. If the sea overtops these sea defences and gets into fragile freshwater habitats, it will kill freshwater and soil invertebrates and affect the birds, such waders which feed on them.

In November 2007, a combination of high tides and a tidal surge flowing down from the northern North Sea resulted in dramatic flooding at Dingle Marshes.

The grazing marshes and freshwater reedbeds are protected from the sea by a natural shingle ridge. The sea breached the shingle ridge in several places, completely flooding the adjacent grazing marshes and overtopping the wall which protects the freshwater marsh. The effect on the landscape was dramatic with sea water surging inland for almost 2km and roads and footpaths being closed.

Out at sea...
Climate change can alter the feeding patterns of fish such as sand eels. A shortage of sand eels is already causing young seabirds, such as those of little terns at several colonies along the Suffolk coast, to starve to death resulting in dramatic population declines.

Heading north-west.
It is predicted that in time many bird species will move as much as 550km north-west from their current range. This could mean that the Suffolk coast is colonized by birds only found at present on mainland Europe, such as cattle egrets and hoopoes. Migratory birds may be affected by climate change on their wintering grounds.

How is the RSPB taking action to adapt to climate change on the Suffolk coast?
The starting premise is to manage existing sites, keeping them in good condition and increasing their size through habitat creation, including linking patches of valuable habitat together. This is landscape-scale conservation and under the Futurescapes initiative the RSPB is working with farmers and landowners to encourage wildlife-friendly practices as part of normal farming activity.

Larger sites are more resistant to the effects of climate change because they provide more opportunities for species to breed and feed, for example birds flooded out of one area can nest on higher ground. Larger sites also allow us to adapt management for new species that might colonise from mainland Europe, while providing habitat for existing species.

By reinforcing sea walls we are protecting the freshwater habitats from sea water. The Environment Agency has just repaired the North Wall at Minsmere which will protect the reserve for many more decades.

Unlike King Knut we have accepted in some places that we have had to let the sea reclaim the land. Where this has happened we have replaced the freshwater habitats that have been lost. New reedbeds at Snape will compensate for losses elsewhere on the Suffolk coast. We have created new intertidal habitats at Havergate by deliberately breaching a small section of river wall.

During the winter months we will store more water which will allow us to re-charge wetlands during the spring and summer. This will make it easier to keep the Minsmere Scrape in tip-top condition for breeding and migrant waders.

We can see that climate change is already having an effect on wildlife on the Suffolk coast. Thanks to your support the RSPB will continue to respond and adapt to the challenges in order to maintain the area as one of the best places for wildlife in the UK.

RSPB

Dingle Marshes & Dunwich Forest

Pioneering partnerships

Suffolk Wildlife Trust

FRAGILE BEAUTY: The North Sea is just yards away from the marshes, which are home to the exciting marsh harrier, inset. The area is sometimes flooded by salt water.

Geography and history

The area of lonely marshland and reedbeds north of Dunwich, known as Dingle Marshes, is steeped in history. One thousand years ago the present marshes formed the shore of a wide bay, Dunwich Haven, with the thriving town of Dunwich and its busy harbour on the southern margin.

In the 12th Century, Dunwich was one of the major East Coast ports but since then the soft sand, clay and pebble cliff, on which the town was built, has been eroded progressively by the encroaching North Sea, taking houses, public buildings and 19 churches under the waves.

Now all that remains of the medieval town are the ruins of Greyfriars Monastery outside the town walls, on the present cliff edge, and the chapel of the leper hospital in the churchyard of St James' church at the end of the village street. The few remaining fishing boats and fishermen's huts on the beach are relics of its rich maritime history.

The Dunwich River is reduced to a slow stream winding north through the marshes to join the River Blyth at Walberswick.

As the sea encroached and the bay silted up, enclosed by a natural shingle ridge, much of the low-lying ground became farmland used for rough grazing. Rising ground to the west remained as Sandlings heath.

At the start of the Second World War some of the water meadows were flooded as a defence measure and, as at Minsmere, the land reverted to reedbed. Much of this remains today and the northern part, Westwood Marshes, is managed as a reserve by Natural England.

Much of the heathland was planted with conifers by the Forestry Commission in the 1950s to create Dunwich Forest. Great and Little Dingle Hills are well-known landfall sites for migrating passerines, some of which are trapped in mist nets and ringed by members of the long-established Dingle Bird Club.

The Dingle Marshes reserve of 258 hectares (ha) is a co-operative venture. It was purchased by the RSPB and the Suffolk Wildlife Trust (SWT) in 1998 and is jointly managed, with a warden from each organisation, in conjunction with Natural England and Dunwich Town Trust. It consists of two contiguous main sections. One, managed by SWT, is the grazing marshes, with the Dunwich River and saline lagoons, inside the shingle ridge.

The other to the north, managed by the RSPB, is the southern segment of the wide valley of the Westwood Marshes reedbed, which runs inland from the old windmill. The remainder of this reedbed is managed by Natural England. On its southern margin the land rises and the reedbed merges with the developing acid grassland and the forest. The acquisition of this reserve formed another link in the chain of coastal wetlands with saltmarsh, reedbeds and lagoons being conserved for wildlife along the Suffolk coast from Lowestoft to Felixstowe. This enables birds and other wildlife to move freely along 'corridors' between different feeding grounds and breeding sites according to the season. The recent work in Dunwich Forest adds another vital link to this chain.

Dingle Marshes is a quiet and remote reserve, deliberately low key, where visitors can use public and permissive footpaths to observe the wildlife in its natural habitat. There is one hide overlooking the reedbed, with access through Forestry Commission land in Dunwich Forest.

Photo: PAUL GREEN

POWER OF THE SEA: An all-important, but slender and vulnerable, shingle bank protects the reserve.

MILL ON THE MARSH: The old mill standing in Westwood Marshes is an iconic feature among the reeds in which bearded tit, inset, is often to be seen. The pictured bird is a smart adult male.

Habitats and management

The reserve is situated in the Suffolk Coast and Heaths Area of Outstanding Natural Beauty and is part of the Suffolk Heritage Coast. The outstanding qualities of the area have been recognised by the wide range of national and international designations applying to the site. It is a Site of Special Scientific Interest, a Special Protection Area, a Special Area of Conservation and a Ramsar site. It forms part of the Suffolk Coast National Nature Reserve, which was designated in 2003 and encompasses 982ha of land from Dingle Marshes in the south to the Hen Reedbeds on the north side of the River Blyth.

The management of Dingle Marshes is perpetuating wildlife-friendly farming methods in the grazing marshes and continuing co-operation with Natural England in Westwood Marshes.

The range of habitats – lowland wet grassland, reedbed, coastal lagoons, saltmarsh, vegetated shingle ridge, woodland and acid grassland – creates the varied conditions which attract 60 species of breeding birds. The site has outstanding potential for all its wildlife to flourish and increase further in diversity in conjunction with suitable management techniques.

Rising sea levels and the historically unstable coastline pose problems for the reserve and the SWT and RSPB wardens. During most winters the soft cliff at Dunwich is further eroded and the shingle ridge at Dingle Marshes is breached. The sea floods into the reserve, causing damage to the populations of freshwater invertebrates and fish.

The RSPB is planning ahead, creating new reedbeds and grazing marshes at other locations further inland, for example at Snape, to replace those which will inevitably be lost when maintaining the shingle ridge is no longer possible. It is also working with the Environment Agency to explore options for more sustainable management of the Dunwich River which is regularly blocked during storm surges.

Dingle Marshes & Dunwich Forest

Reedbed

The Dingle Marshes reedbed is the southern part of Westwood Marshes, the largest freshwater reedbed in England. The larger northern part has been managed since 1972 by Natural England and its predecessors. The acquisition of the southern part by the RSPB allows the area to be considered as a single ecological unit and will be considered as such in this account.

It has developed on marine clays overlain by a thick layer of peat. Looking out over the vast expanses of reeds stretching into the distance, traces of its history can be detected – old gateposts, field boundaries, hedges and ditches survive from its time as grazing pasture.

The marsh supports a specialist community of insects, fish, birds and animals in the mixture of habitats provided by the reeds, the willow and alder fen, the ditches and lagoons. Marsh harriers, bearded tits and bitterns have maintained a presence here for many years and the management programme aims to sustain and enhance their populations.

This is a working, commercial reedbed. It has been traditionally managed with some of the reeds used for thatching. The reeds are cut between November and January. Some sections are cut annually for a period of seven to ten years and then left while other areas are exploited. In addition, some areas of wetter reedbed are cut using a Truxor, an amphibious reed-cutting machine, and other areas of the reedbed are managed by Konik ponies that thrive by grazing on the rough, wet vegetation.

This harvesting, grazing and trampling prevents scrub encroachment and drying out and maintains a good flow of fresh spring water and surface drainage water through the reedbed and lagoons to the 1930s drainage ditches. These have been opened up and widened to create 5m-wide water channels leading to the Dunwich River.

This management has been successful in providing open, wet, reedbed with edges for feeding bitterns. It has also increased the area of open water for wintering and resident wildfowl. The Westwood Marshes reedbed has some protection from potential sea incursions thanks to a secondary earth dam with sluices, inland from the old windmill. Seaward of this bank, the Point Marsh reedbed is becoming gradually more saline.

AMONG THE REEDS: Water rail, main photo, and reed warbler, inset, can be seen in the reedbed.

Main photo: LOWESTOFT LOUNGE LIZARDS, inset: JON EVANS

SUMMER ON THE MARSHES: Lapwings favour the marshland mosaic, while species such as common whitethroat, below, and other warblers nest in the area's small patches of scrub.

Grazing marshes

Looking out over the grazing marshes from the Dunwich village street, the view that you see has changed considerably over the past thousand years. It was once part of the wide estuary and harbour of the Dunwich River which disappeared as the river changed course and the harbour silted up.

Now, in summer, cattle graze in the meadows with swallows and house martins swooping for flies overhead. In winter, ducks and geese roost as the occasional visiting hen harrier quarters the reeds. The management plan revolves around keeping water levels higher in the silt and clay soils than in the recent past, using a series of sluices.

Some of the original creeks have been opened up with mechanical diggers to increase the flow of fresh spring water, flushing through any salt that may have accumulated and to provide more feeding edges for waders. There are small patches of reed and scrub, providing ideal habitats for nesting birds such as mallards, common whitethroats, sedge, grasshopper and reed warblers.

A new scrape, with islands for nesting waders, has been created beyond the Dunwich beach car park. The pasture is kept well grazed by around 250 cattle in the summer. They are moved from field to field to avoid the nesting birds. Rushes in the wet fields and ragwort in the dry fields are mechanically cut to prevent their spread. This creates the mosaic of short grass and tussocks favoured for nesting by lapwings and redshanks respectively.

Dingle Marshes & Dunwich Forest

Dingle Marshes & Dunwich Forest

Foreshore

The history of this coast is one of constant change, with natural movements of sand and shingle. Rising sea levels and increasing frequency of storms, due to climate change, are threatening the freshwater status of Dingle Marshes. Storms, combined with tidal surges, have occurred regularly since 2003, undermining and causing irreparable damage to the shingle ridge.

After the dramatic breach in 2007, the sea surged through the gap in the ridge at each high tide. The decision was then made by the Environment Agency to re-build the ridge at a reduced height. The ridge is now lower but wider, so is less likely to breach as dramatically as in 2007. Instead at the crest of a storm surge, the sea should over-top along the ridge.

This strategy should allow nature to take its course, the ridge gradually moving inland as the shingle is washed over into the saltmarsh and saline lagoons. In the 2011/12 surges the breaches mostly sealed themselves, but excavators were used to dig the shingle out of the Dunwich River, to prevent freshwater flooding further upstream.

The shingle ridge, which extends in a wide sweep from Dunwich to Walberswick, is known for its specialist shingle flora. It holds a European Union designation as a Special Area of Conservation to emphasise the need to protect the striking plants – sea pea, yellow horned-poppy and sea kale – which grow there. Electric fencing protects some of the area, where little terns nest and rear their young, in the spring and summer.

An interesting and rare habitat can be seen behind the shingle ridge. Seepage and incursions of seawater have created saline lagoons surrounded by saltmarsh and shingle.

Unusual invertebrates occur here – brackish water Gammarus shrimps and starlet sea anemones – alongside the abundant minute Hydrobia snails which provide food for the waders which nest on the shingle.

The Dunwich River runs north through the grazing marshes, parallel to the shingle ridge. As the ridge moves inland, this important drainage channel is becoming more susceptible to being blocked by shingle.

The course of the river may be re-routed further away from the sea by channeling the water through existing major drainage ditches in the grazing marshes.

SPECIAL PROTECTION: The tiny little tern, above, is a species that benefits from parts of the Dingle Marshes shingle beach, inset, being fenced off during the breeding season.

Main photo: LOWESTOFT LOUNGE LIZARDS, inset, MALCOLM KEY

Grassland and woodland

The small amount of acid grassland and woodland on the reserve is mostly situated on the gently rising ground formed by the sand and gravel post-glacial deposits of the Sandlings. The developing acid grassland requires careful management. Some of the fields are being grazed by sheep and cattle to create grassland suitable for skylarks, woodlarks and stone-curlews to nest. Other fields are being left to return to scrub, thus providing habitats for common and lesser whitethroats. There is a small section of marshy woodland in Fen Covert. The mixed deciduous woodland needs little management.

IMPRESSIVE INSECT: The white admiral butterfly can be seen in the Dingle and Dunwich woodlands.

Fauna

A varied series of habitats such as this will inevitably support a wide range of other animal species besides birds. Otters have taken advantage of the plentiful supplies of rudd and eels in the reedbed where water voles and water shrews thrive in the ditches despite the occasional predatory mink.

Muntjac stray in from Dunwich Forest and red deer pass through on their way to the reedbed where they create useful tracks, breaking up the dense reeds. Hares can be seen in the grazing marshes, badgers and rabbits burrow in the light, sandy soil in the southern part of the reserve. Foxes are kept out of the grazing marshes and parts of the shingle ridge during the breeding season by electric fencing, thus protecting the eggs and young of the ground-nesting birds.

On warm spring days adders and common lizards may be basking in the sunshine on the path edges. Grass snakes and amphibians

Dingle Marshes & Dunwich Forest

DIVERSITY: Common blue damselfly, main photo, and silver Y moths add to the reserve's interest. The non-native muntjac deer, below, is now widespread in Britain and can frequently be seen at Dingle and Dunwich.

such as toads, frogs and smooth newts have ample territory in the reedbed.

Several species of dragonfly and damselfly can be seen flying in summer as they hatch from the ditches and pools. Hairy dragonflies are followed by southern hawkers and these may be joined by migrant hawkers and four-spotted chasers. The rare Norfolk hawker dragonfly is a recent colonist and common blue, blue-tailed and large red damselflies can all be seen in the summer months.

Butterflies such as white admiral, common and holly blue and small tortoiseshell can be seen feeding on the nectar of flowers at the edges of the woodland rides where speckled wood butterflies rest on the vegetation and, when conditions are favourable, the migrant painted lady appears in substantial numbers. Purple hairstreak and white-letter hairstreak butterflies can also be found in localized places in the deciduous parts of the woodland.

A large number of moths have been recorded on the reserve, among them the rare Fenn's wainscot moth, but the casual observer is more likely to spot one of the day-flying moths such a burnet, migrant silver Y or one of the hawkmoths.

Flora

The most numerous plants on the reserve are adapted to wetland conditions. The huge expanse of reeds in the marshes, changing colour from green to purple and then brown and cream as the seed-heads develop and ripen, is a spectacular sight through the seasons.

Other water plants, such as reedmace and the scarce marsh sow-thistle, grow among the reeds. Spearworts, forget-me-nots and arrowhead grow around the wetland margins and frogbit and the carnivorous bladderwort occur in the ditches.

In the saltmarsh around the saline lagoons, the purple sea aster flowers in July and August.

As the marshes are more frequently inundated with salt water, the gradual change of freshwater grazing marsh to saltmarsh can be visually tracked across the site by the spread of these flowers. The shingle ridge supports patches of rare but locally flourishing shingle-loving plants – the pink sea pea, yellow horned-poppy and sea kale.

Oaks, sycamores and birch dominate the woodland with alder in the wet areas of Fen Covert and willow scrub along the edges of the reedbed.

Wildlife season by season

WINTER: DECEMBER, JANUARY, FEBRUARY

Dingle Marshes reserve contributes to the network of wetlands on the Suffolk coast that provide havens for wintering wildfowl. It provides an alternative feeding area for many waders when the tide is high on the neighbouring River Blyth estuary.

The wet grassland of the grazing marshes provides ideal feeding conditions for ducks and geese which winter here. They are best viewed from the shingle ridge or from the Dingle track along the edge of Dunwich Forest. Up to 1,000 teals may be feeding on seeds in the tussocky vegetation with perhaps 500 to 600 wigeons alongside them and smaller numbers of shelducks, mallards and shovelers. Greylag and Canada geese can be seen in all seasons, but they are joined in winter by varying numbers of white-fronted geese and maybe a few whooper swans.

Flocks of herring and lesser black-backed gulls will visit to feed and roost, together with up to 400 lapwings and groups of redshanks. Smaller numbers of common snipe, and occasionally spotted redshanks, also winter here and can often be picked out as they fly over the pools and ditches. On the shingle alongside the saline lagoons turnstones will feed and move on.

CHARMER: Snow buntings enliven winter days.

A regular flock of twite, sometimes numbering up to 70 birds, feeds on seeds on the shingle. This is the most reliable site in Suffolk for this localized winter visitor. Linnets, goldfinches and snow buntings can frequently be seen among them. A few shorelarks and the occasional Lapland bunting are present in most winters.

From the hide looking over the reedbed, several marsh harriers can often be seen as they hunt for amphibians or small mammals. In the winter months, they may be joined here in the reeds at dusk by other birds of prey, such as hen harriers and merlins in the raptor roost. Visitors can also observe flocks of starlings as they arrive to roost in the reedbed.

With the aid of a telescope, the keen seawatcher may pick out some of Sole Bay's wintering red-throated divers and great crested grebes.

PASSING THROUGH: The turnstone is one of the species of migratory wader that calls in to the reserve.

Spring: March, April, May

The departure of a flock of wintering ducks or geese, or a booming male bittern on a bright February morning, signals the change of season. Numbers of booming, and indeed nesting, bitterns fluctuate in the reedbed depending on the supply of freshwater fish and amphibians as food for the developing young birds. This is often linked to the frequency of saline flooding.

The song of the skylark, the piping display calls of redshanks and the arrival of the first passage migrant waders confirms the arrival of spring. The majority of the lapwings will have departed for their Continental breeding grounds by the end of March, but the 12 or so pairs which remain will be beginning their courtship displays in the grazing marshes.

Redwings and fieldfares gather on the fields in March before flying north, coinciding with the arrival of ring ouzels as they head for the uplands of Britain for the breeding season.

From late March, common and green sandpipers and greenshanks will stay for a time on the edges of the pools in the grazing marshes before moving on. Ruffs, bar-tailed and black-tailed godwits will follow, with turnstones feeding on the shingle by the sea wall. By late April, grey plovers will be passing through and small groups of whimbrels may stay for a time.

On the broad expanse of the grazing marshes, the nesting lapwings and skylarks choose the open ground for their shallow nests. Redshanks prefer the cover of a tussock of rushes and gadwalls, mallards, shovelers and tufted ducks seek out the dense vegetation on the edges of the drainage ditches.

Of the birds that breed on Dingle Marshes, none is more exciting to observe than the marsh harrier. At this time they will frequently be seen, performing their aerial displays, collecting nesting material or hunting over the reedbed. The displays are visible from several of the public footpaths in and around the reserve and especially from the Dingle track viewpoint. The males are polygamous, each one may mate with more than one female. In a good year, there may be as many as ten females with nests in the Westwood Marshes reedbed, rearing over 20 young.

By contrast, water rails are rarely seen. It is estimated that there may be in excess of 100 pairs of these secretive birds in 200ha of reedbed. Their squealing calls can be heard in the early morning from late March to mid-April. The thick scrubby margins of the reedbed are used for nesting by the expanding resident population of Cetti's warblers. An explosive chatter reveals their presence as they feed at the water's edge.

Around the saline lagoons and on the shingle ridge, ringed plovers, avocets, oystercatchers and occasionally little terns nest, their eggs well camouflaged against the shingle stones. These ground-nesting birds are very susceptible to disturbance, by foxes and exceptionally high tides, but the main problem at this time of the year is walkers who stray from the footpath or who allow their dogs to run free. Yellow wagtails may attract our attention in April, but pied wagtails can be seen more frequently as they breed on the reserve. Linnets and stonechats will begin to nest in the scattered patches of gorse on the higher areas.

Most of the summer migrants have returned by the end of April and they will be establishing their territories, alongside the resident species. Reed buntings and bearded tits will be joined by sedge, grasshopper and reed warblers feeding and building their intricately woven nests in the reeds.

In the woodland and hedgerows the territorial singing of songbirds such as blackcaps, chiffchaffs, garden and willow warblers will be heard alongside resident robins, wrens, bullfinches, song thrushes and blackbirds. Common and lesser whitethroats sing from the hawthorns and invisible nightingales sing from the depths of dense vegetation. Green woodpeckers call as they fly off the grassland and the drumming of great spotted woodpeckers resonates through the woodland.

FAMILIAR SIGHTS: The shoveler, main photo, and the blackcap, inset, are regularly seen on the reserve.

Photos: JON EVANS

RARELY SEEN: The glow worm, main photo, and white-letter hairstreak butterfly, inset.

SUMMER: JUNE, JULY, AUGUST

This must be the favourite time of year for many regular visitors to Dingle Marshes. On a still, warm day in mid-summer, looking across the reedbed from near the old windmill, families of bearded tits can be seen flitting through the tops of the reeds, feeding and calling as they move along.

In the distance, a hobby may swoop and turn as it attempts to capture a dragonfly or damselfly over the water. As the dark brown young of the marsh harriers leave the nest they fly and hunt with their parents, but quickly become independent and competent hunters.

From the shingle ridge, common and little terns can be observed as they hover and plunge for fish in the sea or saline lagoons. Look out for scarce flowers such as yellow horned-poppy and sea pea, but take care not to trample them.

By late June, spotted redshanks, greenshanks, bar-tailed and black-tailed godwits, dunlins, green sandpipers and the occasional little stint will be returning to the lagoons on the grazing marshes from breeding grounds further north. At the same time, any ringed plovers and oystercatchers that have bred will leave the reserve to feed on the local estuaries.

Summer is a great time to look for some of Dingle's insects. Dragonflies dart and hawk along the edges of pools, or rest on floating vegetation to lay their eggs. Among the most impressive are the huge emperor dragonflies and the recently arrived Norfolk hawker, but southern hawkers and ruddy darters may be more obvious.

A walk along the woodland track may produce sightings of one of our most striking butterflies, the white admiral, but you'll need to search carefully among the oak canopy to glimpse a purple hairstreak. A few white-letter hairstreaks remain around dead elms close to the reserve's western boundary.

In June and July, an evening walk at dusk along the Dingle track might be rewarded with the sight of glow worms in the short grass and the churring sound of nightjars as they hunt for moths through the clearings in the forest.

Little egrets that breed locally can be seen on the reserve at all times of year, but from August onwards there can be as many as eight individuals feeding here, joined from time to time by a spoonbill.

AUTUMN: SEPTEMBER, OCTOBER, NOVEMBER

From late August onwards, visitors may see migrants arriving or passing through. Wheatears, whinchats, redstarts and pied flycatchers regularly stop to rest and feed in areas of scrub on the reserve and large numbers of meadow pipits pass through during the autumn.

Later, flocks of finches may move through, before the first redwings and fieldfares arrive in October. With so many birds on the move, there's always the chance of a rare visitor such as a wryneck, red-backed shrike or yellow-browed warbler.

Waders are on the move too. Among the commoner species, you may find small flocks of little stints, curlew sandpipers, ruffs or greenshanks, or perhaps even a vagrant from Siberia or North America. Offshore, flocks of ducks may be seen heading south and the parties of brent geese arrive. Look out for skuas, gannets or the odd seal too.

Bearded tits gather into flocks early on October mornings and take off together, spiralling upward to disperse to other wetland areas in the south and west of the UK. Some bearded tits remain here in all months of the year but are vulnerable to hard weather and coastal flooding.

Month by month through the autumn, wintering wildfowl and waders will arrive from the north, gathering on the grazing marshes to roost and feed. There will be little disturbance. Few visitors other than naturalists and those seeking solitude come here in winter. The only sounds will be the crashing of waves on the shingle, the movement of the wind in the reeds and the trees of the forest – and the murmuring and whistling of the birds.

MIGRANTS: Globe-trotting wheatears, main photo, and greenshanks, above, fuel up for their journeys by feeding on the reserve.

Dunwich Forest

Dunwich Forest is an extensive area of coniferous forest, planted by the Forestry Commission on 500ha of Sandlings heath and farmland in the 1950s. Among the densely planted conifers are small patches of deciduous trees and open areas of heather and bracken heathland. With its proximity to the sea and to the RSPB Dingle Marshes and Minsmere reserves, the forest has always been popular with birdwatchers and other visitors, with access on a network of forest tracks. However, much of its potential has been lost as the conifers have matured, reducing the ecological diversity.

In an ambitious project to recreate the original, more open, landscape of the Sandlings, the RSPB and SWT have established a joint enterprise with the Forestry Commission which owns the forest. This is a long-term project – at least 40 years – during which the appearance of Dunwich Forest will gradually be transformed.

GRAZERS: Exmoor ponies are traditional site 'managers'.

The SWT is responsible for the area north of the Dunwich-Blythburgh road where, over a number of years, with felling and natural succession, a broad-leaved forest will develop in the place of the conifers. The aim is to create wood pasture, grazed by Dartmoor ponies, with a mosaic of trees and more open areas with a wider range of flowering plants. This will encourage butterflies such as white admiral and white-letter hairstreak and benefit birds such as warblers and nightingales.

South of the road, on less fertile, sandy and stony soils, the Forestry Commission is already working to clear-fell some of the mature stands of conifers which are ready to be commercially extracted. As the conifers are progressively harvested, the RSPB is taking over the management of the cleared blocks with the aim of re-creating the former heath and acid grassland that existed prior to afforestation. Invasive species such as bracken and brambles are cleared, whilst heather, other heathland plants and grasses such as bent grass and fescues, are encouraged to colonise from the natural seed bank remaining in the soil, augmented by additional seeding where necessary.

Grazing by rabbits, red deer and Exmoor ponies will maintain the developing heathland where Dartford warblers, stonechats and woodlarks should flourish. Along the edges of the remaining stands of deciduous and coniferous trees nightjars will hunt at dusk for the moths on which they feed.

Silver-studded blue and grayling butterflies will also benefit from this work.

Similar projects have been initiated by the RSPB and the Forestry Commission in Rendlesham and Tunstall forests. The work will take place over a similar timescale and the aim is to create a mixture of heathland and woodland, giving an attractive landscape, public access and a diversity of habitats for wildlife. It should be noted that all these forests were planted on what was originally Sandlings heath, which the work is aiming to re-create.

Dunwich Forest is designated as Open Access land and is criss-crossed with rights of way and forest tracks. Access is easy throughout the forest, at all times, although there may be some restrictions during the breeding season to protect rare ground-nesting birds. Dogs, for example, must be kept under effective control at this time, and whenever they are close to grazing livestock.

Reserve reflections: special memories of Dingle Marshes

John Brinkley Easy (may he rest in peace under the sea)

‘My first encounter with John Brinkley Easy was in 1958. I came to Suffolk for the first time with a group of student birdwatching friends. We arrived late, in the dark, guided to the cliff top campsite by one of our number who knew the area and who was to take us to Minsmere the next day. I pitched my tent and settled for the night in my sleeping bag on the hard ground. Then followed the most uncomfortable night of my life – sinister dreams alternated with waking and listening fearfully to the sound of the sea below us. I woke as the sun rose out of the sea and saw the amazing view from our position perched on the cliff edge. Only then did I look to the side of the tent and see the solitary tomb stone and the grave on which my tent was pitched.

There was the inscription:

SACRED
To the Memory of
JOHN BRINKLEY EASY
1826
23 Years

When I returned to Dunwich twenty years later I discovered the story of Dunwich, the city under the sea and the churchyard of All Saints Church where John Easy had been buried. The grave was much nearer to the edge of the cliff as the waves and storms had taken their toll of the soft rock. Since then the tombstone and the cliff top campsite have all been swept into the sea and I do not know what happened to John Brinkley Easy.’

Jenny James
RSPB Woodbridge Local Group volunteer

RSPB — Pioneering partnerships — Suffolk Wildlife Trust

RESERVE INFORMATION

How to get there

From the A12 via Westleton or Blythburgh to Dunwich village.

Opening times

Access at all times on public and permissive footpaths only. The circular walk heads north along the shingle ridge from Dunwich for almost two miles before cutting inland on a low bank towards the Westwood Marshes Mill. Before the windmill, turn left past Dingle Great Hill to pick up the forest track back to Dunwich. The full circuit is about five miles.

Facilities

- Park at Dunwich Beach car park for the circular walk; use the northern Dunwich Forest car park on the Dunwich/Blythburgh road for the hide; use the car park on the Walberswick/Blythburgh road for Westwood Marshes.
- Information boards for guidance on trails.
- One hide overlooking Westwood Marshes with access through Dunwich Forest.
- Café, tea room and public house in Dunwich village.
- Toilets at beach car park.
- For wheelchair access, the Dingle track along the edge of the Dunwich Forest is firm but with an uneven surface. It may be muddy and rutted particularly after wet weather.

Further Information

Contact: RSPB Minsmere, tel 01728 648281; email: minsmere@rspb.org.uk or see www.rspb.org.uk/dinglemarshes
Contact: SWT, tel: 01473 890089; or see www.suffolkwildlifetrust.org

Minsmere

A magical mosaic

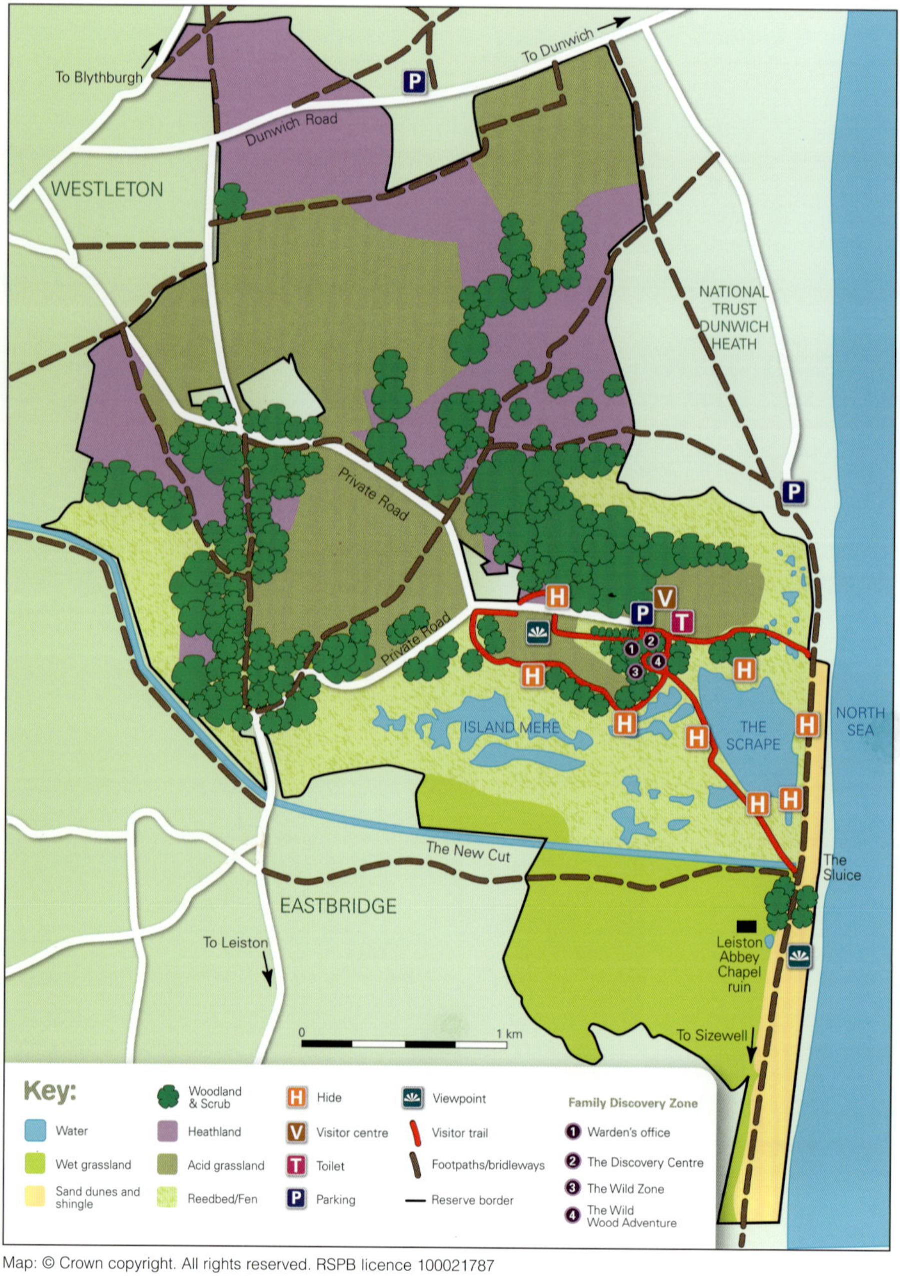

A NEW DAY DAWNS: Sunrise at Minsmere. The reserve is justifiably famous for its populations of several species, including bittern, inset.

Geography and history

Minsmere's wetlands have changed markedly over the years. Historically the winding Minsmere River opened into an estuary and flowed to the sea at Minsmere Haven. After repeated flooding, the river was modified and the New Cut dug to improve the drainage of the Minsmere valley.

Eventually the area was protected from the sea by a clay bank, inland from the dunes, allowing the land to be reclaimed. By the 1930s it had developed into a patchwork of grazing marshes and reed-filled ditches, which were rich in plant and animal life and supported a wide variety of birds.

At the beginning of the Second World War, parts of the East Anglian coast were flooded as a defence against invasion. At Minsmere, the sea sluices were opened until a brackish mixture of water covered much of the low-lying area of the original estuary.

The reeds spread and flourished in the flooded meadows and, by the end of the war, over 150 hectares (ha) of land had been transformed into shallow, brackish and freshwater meres and marsh surrounded by reedbeds.

This simple act of flooding had, by chance, created the beginnings of one of the UK's best-loved nature reserves. Plans from before the war were revived, resulting in a leasing agreement between the owner, Captain Stuart Ogilvie, and the RSPB in April 1947. The RSPB finally purchased the reserve in 1977 following an appeal to its members who helped to meet the asking price of £250,000.

The reserve was originally part of the Scott's Hall Estate and contained mixed woodland with wide rides and coverts around the edge of wet meadows. Gamekeepers controlled predators and so promoted wildlife diversity by providing cover and food resources, and by protecting nests and young birds from predation.

In those early days the reserve consisted of

FROM UP ON HIGH: Reedbeds, lagoons, woodland and part of the Levels that help make up the mosaic.

620ha, comprising reedbeds and lagoons, with higher ground to the north covered by Sandlings heath and mixed woodland. The eastern margin was along the sea wall from the Coastguard Cottages on Dunwich Cliffs in the north to Minsmere Sluice, where the New Cut enters the sea, about a mile to the south. The southern boundary followed the New Cut westward to Eastbridge, about a mile inland.

Recent purchases by the RSPB have added three blocks of farmland on the reserve's northern periphery and an area of grazing marsh, known as the Levels, south of the New Cut.

It is here that the evocative ruins of the original Leiston Abbey, founded in 1182, can be seen. In 1363 however, after disastrous floods, the abbey was dismantled. Only the chapel was left, the remains of which are now a much-loved feature of the Levels. Recent work to repair collapsed walls, funded by English Heritage and Natural England, should secure this historic building's future.

Within its current boundaries, Minsmere embraces an unusual mosaic of habitats which includes most of those found in other parts of lowland England. These include reedbeds, shallow lagoons, woodland, heathland, wet grassland, acid grassland, farmland and a coastal dune system behind a shingle-and-sand beach.

The history of the reserve is inextricably linked to the avocet, a species which was lost as a British breeding bird in the mid-19th Century. Just as the Minsmere leasing agreement was being signed in 1947 rumours began to spread of the return of the 'awl bird'.

Local people had seen four birds on the Minsmere marshes, which remained flooded

MUCH-LOVED: The old abbey ruins on the Levels.

following the Second World War. This was a time when such spectacular birds were at risk from egg collectors and taxidermists, so secrecy was paramount. The birds, code-named 'zebras', were watched over by volunteers. Four nests were found and by early June the first young avocets in the UK for over 100 years had hatched on a muddy islet.

Avocets did not breed again at Minsmere until 1963 due to the re-vegetation of open waters and muddy fringes. Fortunately a successful colony of over 100 pairs built up at nearby Havergate Island, where they also nested in 1947, and this too became an RSPB nature reserve.

Since 1947, the Minsmere reserve has developed and grown thanks to the devotion of a series of wardens, whose love of birds and skill as habitat 'engineers' combined to create today's 980ha-reserve.

The first part-time warden, Dick Wolfendale, lived in a tent on wages of £1.00 per week. Only eight weekly visitors were allowed. The wildlife and a band of enthusiastic volunteers had the reserve to themselves. In those magical early days, bitterns, bearded tits, redstarts, nightingales, wheatears, red-backed shrikes, nightjars, stone-curlews and many more nested in the rich variety of habitats already on the reserve.

RETURN TO BRITAIN: The iconic avocet, rightly chosen as the RSPB's logo bird.

The first hides were made of driftwood, with ex-Army corrugated iron roofs. A pioneering idea in 1948 was the provision of a public hide on the Scrape side of the sea wall, a revised version of which, a viewing platform, exists today. Driftwood from the tideline was also used to make nestboxes and the first noticeboards, gates, bridges and boardwalks on the wet and muddy marsh paths.

In 1959 Bert Axell became the reserve's first full-time warden. By 1962 he had begun to create the first artificial 'scrape'. Bert's innovative management work set the standard which has been maintained through succeeding decades. Indeed, scrapes of a similar design to that at Minsmere have since been constructed at many wetland nature reserves around the world.

The reserve has been at the forefront of the RSPB's research programme on habitat management and restoration, on strategies for halting the decline of threatened species, in particular marsh harriers, bitterns, nightjars and stone-curlews, and on breeding waders and predator control.

Over the years Minsmere has grown with the RSPB. In 1959 there were 624 visitors. By 2012 this had grown to 90,000. Today Minsmere is one of the RSPB's 'flagship' reserves, showing how people and wildlife can co-exist.

There is a core group of full-time RSPB staff. They are assisted by volunteers who help at the visitor centre, lead guided walks, work at the reception desk, shop and café, and carry out management and survey work. There is a series of nature trails with hides within the reserve and a network of public rights of way around the perimeter. The hides have been renewed and enlarged over the years to improve viewing and to give disabled people access

PROTECTING THE RESERVE: The new North Wall, which ensures Minsmere's future is free from flood risk.

A major part of the Minsmere Discover Nature Project, supported by the Heritage Lottery Fund, the EU and other funders, is a new Discovery Centre. Here school groups can enjoy an exciting programme of outdoor learning with the new Learning Manager and team of RSPB Field Teachers. The Discovery Centre is also used for art exhibitions and workshops, illustrated talks and family craft events.

Alongside the Discovery Centre is the new Wild Zone where families and school groups can learn through play with a series of fun exhibits including a child-sized sand martin bank and den-making.

wherever possible. The Bittern hide is built high above the reedbed with impressive views over the reserve. The spacious new Island Mere hide takes birdwatchers right into the reedbed, close to the feeding bitterns and the wintering ducks, geese and swans on the lagoons.

In 2012 the RSPB completed a major upgrade of visitor facilities and interpretation at Minsmere to help make the reserve even more attractive to visitors. The café has been enlarged and the shop reorganised, with a new reception area providing a much-improved welcome to the reserve.

Also completed in 2012 was the Environment Agency's Minsmere Coastal Defence Project. This involved rebuilding the North Wall into a full sea defence bank, which will protect the reserve's precious freshwater habitats from rising sea levels and winter storms.

The dunes have been eroded by storm surges on several occasions since 2005, threatening the future of the North Marsh reedbed. While this part of the reserve will, in time, become more brackish, the remaining reedbed and the Scrape are now secure.

ROOM WITH A VIEW: The new Island Mere hide allows close encounters with wildlife as well as panoramic views across the reedbed and beyond.

PIONEERING CREATION: The famous Scrape – a vision turned into reality by Bert Axell.

Habitats and management

Situated on the Suffolk Heritage Coast, Minsmere is part of the Suffolk Coast & Heaths Area of Outstanding National Beauty. It holds a Council of Europe Diploma – one of only five sites in the UK to do so. It is a Site of Special Scientific Interest, a Ramsar site, a Special Protection Area, a Special Area of Conservation and a Wildlife Heritage Site. Management work is funded from a range of sources including the Government agri-environment programme.

The reserve has been continuously managed since the 1960s to provide the widest possible variety of habitats. As a result, more than 5,300 different species have been identified at Minsmere, the highest total for any RSPB nature reserve. Of these, about 340 are bird species with about 90 species breeding each year. On any one day, especially in late spring, it is possible for keen birdwatchers to record up to 100 species on the reserve.

The key to this fantastic success is a healthy and varied environment. All of the habitats now on the reserve were there naturally at some stage in its history. However, the living world is in the process of constant change and if the habitats were left untended the character of the reserve would alter radically. Getting the balance between natural succession and intensive management correct is the result of years of careful management and monitoring by RSPB wardens.

WINTER VISITOR: A smart adult drake smew.

The Scrape

The famous Minsmere Scrape is an artificial habitat designed to re-create the important coastal lagoons which were found widely around the East Anglian coast prior to the construction of sea walls.

In natural conditions, the daily sweep of tides and annual flooding renews the nutrients in these coastal lagoons, making them potentially among the most prolific of wild environments. They are rich in populations of freshwater and brackish-water invertebrates such as minute Hydrobia snails, Corophium brine shrimps, Chironomid midge larvae and water boatmen, on which many wetland birds feed.

As wartime flooding slowly receded, Minsmere's lagoons dried out and became increasingly unsuitable for breeding terns and migrant waders. When Minsmere's first full-time warden, Bert Axell, arrived in 1959 he had a vision to re-create this important habitat. Work began in 1962, with bulldozers scraping shallow hollows into the clay just inside the sea wall. Once flooded, these pools were a mix of fresh water and brackish water, dotted with low gravel islands on which gulls, terns and waders nest.

Being an artificial habitat, the Scrape requires intensive management to mimic the natural processes that make coastal lagoons so important. RSPB wardens have spent 50 years refining this management technique. They can control water levels and salinity by opening sluices and pipes to move water onto, or off, the Scrape, as required.

The ideal management keeps water levels high in winter. In spring, water levels are dropped to expose nesting islands and reduce the risk of flooding the nests. By late summer the Scrape should be largely soft mud, which is ideal for waders' beaks to probe for food, before levels gradually rise in autumn. During recent droughts it has not always been possible to find enough water in summer to keep these muddy areas wet enough for waders.

In recent years wardens have been fallowing part of the Scrape each summer in order to replicate the intermittent flooding that naturally occurs in coastal lagoons. One section of the Scrape is deliberately dried out and re-vegetated. This vegetation is then rotovated to return the nutrients to the ecosystem before the pool is re-flooded.

BACK TO BREED: Avocets have bred at Minsmere every year since 1963, having re-colonised in 1947 after an absence from Britain of more than 100 years.

Minsmere

SEEN ON THE SCRAPE: Main photo, Sandwich terns are frequent visitors, as are greenshanks, top left, curlew sandpipers, top right, ruffs, left, and diminutive little stints, below.

REEDBED SPECIALIST: Minsmere holds a significant percentage of the UK's population of bitterns, and views of the species such as this are often to be enjoyed from the reserve's hides and trails.

Reedbed

Minsmere's freshwater reedbeds, of 179ha, form the third largest block of this habitat in England. The largest is Westwood Marshes, part of which is in the RSPB Dingle Marshes reserve.

Typical reedbed species at Minsmere include bittern, marsh harrier, bearded tit, otter, water vole and several rare wainscot moths, including the white-mantled wainscot which is found in the UK only in the reeds of the mid-Suffolk coast.

Alarm at the collapse of the UK's bittern population during the 1980s resulted in research involving fitting young birds with lightweight radio transmitters. Tracking showed that bitterns prefer the wetter, less dense reedbeds and reedbed margins with several centimetres of water so they can fish from cover for their preferred food species of rudd, sticklebacks and eels which swim freely between widely spaced reed stems.

A management programme followed, in which the reedbed was 're-wetted' by lowering the ground levels by up to one metre using mechanical diggers. New pools were created and ditches cleared to provide refuges for fish and ideal feeding areas for bitterns.

Small areas are cut annually both by hand and by the Truxor, an amphibious reed-cutting machine, which cuts and collects the reeds. This helps to maintain a varied structure within the reedbed. Highland cattle and Konik ponies help to keep the reedbed more open as they graze and trample along the edges.

The Konik is a breed which is a modern Polish re-creation of the original European wild horse, known as the Tarpan. They have mouse-coloured coats and a black stripe down their back. They are long-lived and hardy and will graze on rough, wet areas – making them ideal for wetland management.

The bittern population has responded rapidly to these habitat improvements and the subsequent improved management of reedbeds elsewhere. From a low point of just 11 booming males in the UK in 1997, there were 105 males in 2011, including an incredible 11 males at Minsmere alone.

MANAGEMENT AND RESULTS: Bearded tit, left, is one of the species that benefits from habitat work carried out to keep the reedbeds in good condition. The work involves the use of the Truxor machine, above. Below left, a marsh harrier carries nest material over the main reedbed, below.

Sandlings heath

Minsmere contains an important relic of the Suffolk Sandlings – heathland which originally extended from Lowestoft to Felixstowe. Important heathland species include woodlark, nightjar, stone-curlew, Dartford warbler, natterjack toad, silver-studded blue butterfly and the rare predatory insect, the antlion.

The heathland is a mixture of open areas of acid grassland, heather, gorse and bracken with scattered patches of pine, oak and birch trees. There are also larger areas of mixed deciduous and coniferous woodland.

A fall in the nightjar population to just six pairs in 1980 prompted clearance of invasive birch, pine and oak saplings on the heath. New glades on the woodland edge were created to enable nightjars to hunt moths along the tree margins. Nightjar numbers responded positively to this management and also benefited from the tree clearances caused by the 1987 gale. They are now widespread in suitable habitats.

A pioneering experiment to restore the original Sandlings heath on former farmland is under way. In 1989, 192ha of arable land were bought from the Ogilvie estate, of which 158ha, including a section of coniferous woodland, are being reverted to acid grassland and heath. This involves continued cutting and clearing of vegetation to deplete the soil of nutrients.

Some fields were sown with grasses such as bents and fescues and, where heather was planned, the fields were planted with cuttings from local heaths, while others regenerated naturally. All this was aided by close-grazing by the local rabbits and the RSPB's grazing animals. Most of these are rare breeds such as Manx Loghtan and Wiltshire horn sheep and Exmoor ponies – all very hardy and suitable for coarse grazing.

The aim of these measures was to encourage re-colonisation by stone-curlews, which need low vegetation and patches of bare ground. After 35 years' absence, stone-curlews returned to breed at Minsmere in 2003 and by 2011 there were seven pairs nesting on the reserve. As a highly sensitive species it is not yet possible to arrange public viewing, although post-breeding flocks can sometimes be seen from Westleton Heath in the autumn.

WELCOME RETURNS: Main photo, stone-curlews are now regular breeders on the reserve after an absence of 35 years. Inset, Dartford warblers have also made a comeback to the Suffolk coast and can be seen on the heaths at Minsmere.

Main photo: JON EVANS, inset, BEN HALL (rspb-images.com)

Woodland

In the mixed deciduous woodland, coppicing is maintaining the diversity of breeding birds and encouraging nightingales by creating a mixture of dense understorey and open spaces. New oaks are being planted and old dead trees are left in place to provide feeding and nesting habitat for woodpeckers. Beetles and other insects colonise decaying trees and fallen branches, thereby providing food for woodland birds.

Reserve reflections: special memories of Minsmere

RECOVERING WELL: Silver birch trees are thriving after the devastation of 1987's infamous October storm.

The Storm

Waking on Friday 16 October 1987, the light poured into my bungalow on the Minsmere reserve. Too much light. I looked out of the window and realised that I had slept soundly through a terrible storm, one that had felled many of the great oaks surrounding my home. I went into the kitchen. No electric power, a state of affairs that was to last for nearly three weeks.

Outside, the strong smell of crushed leaves hung in the air as I walked with my colleagues, Rob Macklin and Ian Robinson, to inspect the damage. Mature oak and beech trees blocked the roads out of the reserve, but worse was the fate of our magnificent avenue of lime trees lining the road to Eastbridge – nearly 50 trees down in not much more than 100 yards. Very emotional feelings stated to well up inside.

Altogether we found that we had some 300 mature trees to clear from the two roads leading out of the reserve. Fortunately I was trained to use a chainsaw and so, with Rob and Ian heading teams of volunteers, we began moving the felled trees. This continued until the Monday morning when Rob and Ian took over the chainsaw work. By then I was nearly crippled with severe aching in my arms due to the sustained use of the chainsaw. In fact, for some years after, I was troubled with both tennis and golfer's elbow in both arms.

Aerial photographs established that over 3,000 trees had come down on the reserve. So was it a disaster? My first reaction was that it was, but in the end it proved to be more of an environmental event. Bird populations were not dramatically changed and flora and fungus species actually increased. In the woods we found that many trees had been spared. Today, the scars on the face of our beautiful reserve are healing well.

***Jeremy Sorensen,** Senior Warden,*
Minsmere, 1975 – 1991

Grazing marshes

The 138ha of wet grassland south of the New Cut, known as the Minsmere Levels, are of national importance for wintering wildfowl species, including white-fronted goose, gadwall, teal and wigeon. This is an important area for breeding lapwings and redshanks and wintering common snipe.

The marshes are botanically very rich and also support many species of dragonfly. One of the best areas for plants is a little-known and seldom-visited corner near Eastbridge known as Meadow Marsh.

Management involves control of flood and ditch water levels to create large areas of standing water during the winter months. Grazing by Konik ponies and Highland cattle, hay-making and rush control help to create a patchwork of short swards and rough tussocky grass favoured by waders and other ground-nesting birds.

THREE OF A KIND: A trio of Konik ponies appear to be enjoying their habitat management work.

Foreshore

The Suffolk coast is one of only four areas in the UK with a large expanse of vegetated shingle, making this one of the most significant habitats on the reserve. This is a harsh environment to which several species of salt-tolerant plants are uniquely adapted.

The area is important for recreation so there is inevitable conflict between human access and conservation. Temporary fencing is used to exclude people from certain areas to encourage the establishment of fragile vegetation. Electric fencing is also erected annually in an attempt to protect a vulnerable little tern colony. Despite provision of cover for nests and chicks, this colony has had little breeding success in recent years.

Rising sea levels, and the increase in surge tides associated with climate change, have taken their toll on the dunes. There has been extensive erosion, especially in the northern section, as the dunes are prevented from 'rolling back' to a new location further inland by the secondary defences behind them. The recent Environment Agency work to upgrade the North Wall ensures that most of Minsmere's freshwater habitats will remain protected long after the northern dunes are eroded and North Marsh becomes more saline.

Fauna

As would be expected in such a varied habitat, Minsmere has populations of several small mammals, including water vole – a species threatened in many areas but present here and helped by the reedbed management work. Otters were reintroduced in the 1980s and are now regularly seen in the reedbed pools, especially during the winter.

Several species of bat are commonly seen, including Daubenton's, which hunts over water, noctule, pipistrelle and brown long-eared. It is likely that many of these breed here.

Over 400 red deer flourish throughout the reserve. The dramatic rutting of the stags as they gather their harems of females together is a major attraction in the autumn. The only other species of deer that is usually seen at Minsmere is the diminutive muntjac.

Mammalian predators include badgers, foxes, stoats and weasels, all of which are widespread, although badgers are only likely to be seen at dusk.

Natterjack toad, a rare heathland species, is an interesting introduction. Common frogs and toads breed in profusion in the lagoons alongside smooth and palmate newts. Adders can be seen sunning thyselves on the heath. Grass snakes, slow worms and common lizards also breed on the reserve

A wide variety of common butterflies abound in summer and many of these feed on buddleia and other plants around the reserve. Peacocks, red admirals, small tortoiseshells, commas, gatekeepers and migrant painted ladies can be seen at different times in summer feeding on a range of nectar-producing flowers.

Many grassland butterflies are widespread

Photos: JON EVANS

DRAMATIC DEER: A red deer stag bellows during the spectacular late-autumn rut.

THRILLING ENCOUNTER: Minsmere has become one of the best sites in the UK to see otters.

in areas of short acid or wet grassland or along the dunes. These include Essex, small and large skippers, small coppers, brown argus, green hairstreaks, orange tips, ringlets, meadow browns, common and holly blues and important populations of graylings. Wall browns have sadly disappeared in recent years, mirroring a national decline in this attractive butterfly.

Minsmere's heathland is one of the top sites in Suffolk for silver-studded blue butterflies, which feed on bell heather nectar. The larvae feed on the leaves of heather and gorse and, in an intriguing relationship, the pupae are carried by black ants into their underground nesting tunnels from whence they emerge as adults.

SPECIALITIES: Left, the Minsmere crimson underwing moth which has been named after the reserve and, below, the white-mantled wainscot moth is another major rarity.

In the woodland white admirals have established an expanding colony and purple emperors are occasionally seen. On late summer afternoons purple hairstreaks flutter around the higher foliage of the oak trees.

More than 1,000 species of moth have been identified at Minsmere, thanks to regular use of a moth trap by wardens and volunteers. Some of these moths are day-flying species so may be seen by the casual visitor. Among these are the impressive hummingbird hawkmoth, a regular visitor to buddleias in summer, and the black and red cinnabar and burnet moths.

Several interesting and rare moths breed in the reedbeds, including white-mantled wainscot moth and Fenn's wainscot moth, both of which only breed in the UK on the Suffolk coast. A new species for the UK was found at Minsmere in 2004 and given the English name Minsmere crimson underwing – the first time a species has been named after an RSPB reserve.

The wet areas are ideal for damselflies and dragonflies that breed in the lagoons and ditches. Many of the common British species of hawker, darter, chaser, skimmer and damselflies are present. The rare Norfolk hawker dragonfly is now resident, having until recently been restricted to the Norfolk Broads. Small red-eyed damselflies have also colonised recently. Willow emerald damselflies have been seen on the reserve and should soon become resident.

Photo: MALCOLM FARROW

On warm days in dry, gravelly areas of the dunes, lesser cockroaches, rare coastal insects, may be running and flying around and in more grassy places wasp spiders spin their webs. In the grassland, the loud and varied rasping notes of crickets and grasshoppers fill the air and, as darkness falls, glow worms become visible on the heaths.

Minsmere's other rare and famous insect is the antlion, which was first found breeding in the UK at Minsmere in the 1990s and has only recently been found away from the Suffolk coast. Their large-jawed larvae give the species its name. They lie in wait for ants and other insects in pitfall traps dug in the light, sandy soil. Clusters of pitfall traps can be seen on warm, sandy banks on the heathland and near the visitor centre. The adults are nocturnal so are occasionally attracted to moth traps.

Photo: ROBIN HARVEY

BEAUTY AND THE BEAST: Above, the silver-studded blue butterfly can be seen on Minsmere's heaths. Left, the rare and somewhat curious antlion, whose larvae use cunning to prey on ants and other insects in pitfall traps dug in the light, sandy soils at Minsmere.

TINY POPULATION: The round-leaved wintergreen grows unobtrusively near Island Mere hide.

Flora

On the heaths, Western gorse and European gorse flower throughout the year. Contrasting patches of the first heather, the bright purple bell heather, are in flower by June, followed later by the full glory of the purple ling, or common heather, which colours wide areas of the open heath and fills the air with its scent and yellow pollen.

Minsmere is one of the few places in Britain where red-tipped cudweed occurs, producing its inconspicuous flowers in July and August. Look for it in a small fenced area next to the Bittern hide.

In the reedbeds the *Phragmites* reed covers huge areas, its purple seedheads

LOCALLY PROLIFIC: Marsh mallow blooms along the damp edges of Minsmere's visitor trails bringing a splash of pink to the pathway verges and providing nectar for butterflies.

of late summer turning paler through the autumn and winter. Among the few other species found within the reedbed is the rare marsh sow-thistle and by mid-summer the southern marsh orchid and the yellow iris are found in favoured places in reedbed margins.

Later, marsh mallow, great willowherb and hemp agrimony will be in bloom along the damp edges of the visitor trails. In 2007 a tiny population of round-leaved wintergreen was discovered near Island Mere hide. This was the first Suffolk record for almost 100 years.

The wetlands support a rich range of flowering plants. In early summer, the small white flowers of the water crowfoot and the yellow of the lesser spearwort are overshadowed by water plantain and arrowhead.

The shingle beach and dunes support rare and salt-tolerant plants including the pink sea pea, sea restharrow, yellow horned-poppy and sea kale. These grow in the shingle, obtaining fresh water from deep below the surface with their extensive root systems.

Photo: JENNY JAMES

SUMMER SPLENDOUR: Southern marsh orchid, right, and yellow iris, below, are found in reedbed margins.

Photo: IAN BARTHORPE

Wildlife season by season

WINTER: DECEMBER, JANUARY, FEBRUARY

A winter visit to Minsmere, for those who can withstand the East Coast weather, is a most exciting and rewarding experience. The most favourable times are when the wind is from the north or east and when it is coldest on the Continent. The Scrape, reedbeds and grazing marshes are managed so that they are rich sources of food for energy-hungry birds at the coldest times of the year.

From December onwards, the reserve is a nationally important haven for wintering wildfowl, with flocks of up to 500 white-fronted geese, 2,200 teals, 350 gadwalls, 200 shovelers and 1,500 wigeons. Many of these are on the grazing marshes of the Minsmere Levels. Sometimes they are barely visible in the distance but, when disturbed, clouds of birds rise up and circle round in swirling flocks before disappearing again as they settle back to their feeding and roosting on the ground.

Also wintering on the grazing marshes, though again often well hidden, are good numbers of wetland species such as common snipe, jack snipe, lapwing and redshank. Small numbers of ruffs and dunlins may also over-winter.

Visitors can see these birds most easily, although in smaller numbers, from the hides surrounding the Scrape. Watching birds on the Scrape is one of the highlights of the Minsmere experience at any time of year.

With binoculars or a telescope the birds can be closely observed and their plumage patterns seen in magnificent detail. On a good day groups of teals, gadwalls, shovelers, wigeons and pintails mingle with waders such as redshanks, ruffs, dunlins, lapwings and curlews.

To see some of the wildfowl species wintering on the reserve it is best to look out over the reedbeds and lagoons from Island

Photos: JON EVANS

GRACEFUL VISITORS: Bewick's swans, main photo, and pintail, inset, arrive from the north.

Mere or Bittern hides. Here, among the tufted ducks, goldeneyes and pochards, the ducks to look out for are smews. The female or immature male smews, known as redheads, are more numerous than the males, whose striking black and white breeding plumage earns them the nickname of white nuns. A search of the duck flocks may be rewarded with the discovery of a scarcer species, such as ferruginous duck or green-winged teal.

A small but significant flock of Bewick's swans spends the winter at Minsmere, often accompanied by a few of the larger whooper swans. They usually spend the day grazing on arable fields inland and return to roost overnight on Island Mere. It is a memorable experience to be at Island Mere hide at dusk and to hear the haunting calls of these beautiful birds as they fly in over the reedbeds.

REDHEAD: Female or immature male smews lack the adult male's black and white contrast.

Among the commoner woodland birds, look out for winter visitors such as bramblings, siskins, redwings and fieldfares. With northerly or easterly winds there may also be scarcer visitors around the reserve, such as firecrests and waxwings in the wood and scrub areas and shorelarks and snow buntings in the dunes.

Many of the birds for which Minsmere is justly famous can be seen at all seasons, although there can be some winter dispersal to other wetlands in the UK or further south. Marsh harriers can be seen over the marshes throughout the winter.

These are predominantly females and young birds. The males, and many of the young, head south to spend the winter in the milder climate of Spain or north-west Africa. Bearded tits also range widely during the winter, but pairs or groups of birds are usually to be seen in the reserve reedbeds. On still, bright winter days their 'pinging' calls attract attention as they feed on seeds in the tops of the pale winter reeds.

Minsmere's reedbeds are one of the best places in the UK to look for the rare penduline tit feeding among the reedmace. Small numbers visit in some winters – and springs – but they can be tricky to spot. A British record count of seven was found in 2010.

Bitterns can sometimes be seen feeding in the reedbed margins, or flying low above the reeds. Their superb camouflage helps hide them in the golden winter reedbed, but they may emerge to feed close to Bittern or Island Mere hides, especially in freezing weather. However, by mid-February their haunting foghorn-like booming might be heard across the marshes.

Kingfishers dive from vantage points by the ditches and water rails frequent the reedbeds, though they are often more easily heard than seen. Also wintering here is a small but highly significant number of water pipits. They can sometimes be seen on the Scrape, the Levels or at Island Mere.

Winter is by far the best time to see otters at Minsmere, with family parties often seen on Island Mere or around any of the reedbed pools. Although sightings have become more frequent in recent years, you'll need a lot of luck to spot one.

Look out during winter for a variety of other predators. Barn owls often emerge at dusk, especially towards Eastbridge, while a panic among the ducks may signal the presence of a sparrowhawk or peregrine. Other

EYE OF THE PREDATOR: Sparrowhawks often create panic among the ducks on the reserve.

species that may be spotted, with a bit of luck, include hen harrier, merlin or short-eared owl.

Seawatching can be very rewarding at this time of year as there are many visiting species from cold, northern waters. The best vantage points are Dunwich Cliffs and the dunes near Minsmere Sluice.

Sole Bay holds the UK's largest group of wintering red-throated divers – up to 4,000 birds – and at times hundreds can be seen flying fast and low over the waves. They are taking advantage of the relatively mild conditions and easy feeding, following the sprat shoals in the shallow water over Sizewell Banks. Among the divers are great crested grebes, which have a winter population here of up to 700.

Other species which may be present in much smaller numbers offshore include common scoter, guillemot and kittiwake, while there's always the chance of spotting something much scarcer, such as a pomarine skua or velvet scoter.

Spring can begin to arrive in mid-February with the first booming bittern or the distinctive song of an over-wintering chiffchaff. On sunnier mornings, woodlarks begin their territorial singing over the heaths, an early butterfly or bumblebee may emerge from hibernation, and snowdrops appear along the roadside. The pipistrelle bats or adders may also emerge on warm February days.

SPRING: MARCH, APRIL, MAY

From late February and early March onwards, avocets, lapwings and redshanks begin their courtship displays and prepare to nest on the Scrape. At the same time, the number of wintering birds is diminishing as they start to move north to their breeding grounds.

The first migrants to arrive will usually be chiffchaffs, closely followed by sand martins, whose numbers build up as they begin to investigate the sandy cliff near the visitor centre. Ring ouzels, wheatears and black redstarts also pass through on their way north as the number of passage migrants increases throughout March.

This is a good time to see reptiles and amphibians. Frogs and toads spawn throughout the reedbed and other waterways. On sunny days adders and lizards bask in sunny patches on the heath and grass snakes and slow worms emerge from the undergrowth when disturbed.

On the Scrape, in April and May, noisy black-headed gulls, diving common terns and various waders are jostling for nesting territory. Avocets are guarding their nests, each one a sparsely-lined scrape with four beige and brown mottled eggs, camouflaged as in most ground-nesting birds.

A careful survey of the black-headed gulls may reveal a nesting Mediterranean gull. Up to 40 of these attractive gulls, which do actually have black heads, unlike the misleadingly named black-headed gull, may be present on the Scrape, with a few pairs remaining to breed. Another Minsmere highlight is the spoonbill, a frequent visitor to the Scrape at this time.

Among the migrating waders visiting the Scrape there are many black-tailed godwits and dunlins, with smaller numbers of curlew sandpipers, knots, turnstones, grey plovers and bar-tailed godwits. A few ruffs, with the beginnings of their striking summer plumage, may practice their courtship 'lek' before departing.

Overhead an osprey may be soaring, perhaps lingering long enough to plunge into one of the meres to catch a fish. Red kites and common buzzards are increasingly frequent spring migrants, with several of the latter often seen together. Common cranes

Main photo: JOHN BRIDGES (rspb-images.com), inset, JON EVANS

SIGNS OF SPRING: Cuckoo, main photo, and sand martin, inset, are milestones as the seasons turn.

are usually seen at some point during the spring. These may be Continental birds straying across the North Sea en route from Spain to Sweden, but are perhaps more likely to be birds wandering from the small population that breeds in the Norfolk Broads.

Keen birdwatchers keeping their eyes on the skies for migrants have picked out many rare visitors in recent years. These may include great white egrets, purple herons, white storks, black kites, alpine swifts, red-rumped swallows, or even a bee-eater. A lesser kestrel, in March 2010, was the first one ever seen in Suffolk.

During April and May the reserve is traditionally at its best and the return of the summer migrants reaches its peak. Many of the woodland birds arrive in sequence and can be detected by their songs. The chiffchaffs are followed in late March by the first willow warblers and as April progresses blackcaps and nightingales return. These are followed by garden warblers in the woods and whitethroats and lesser whitethroats in the scrubby areas.

ONE TO WATCH FOR: Great white egret is now a regular visitor to the reedbeds and levels.

A few pairs of redstarts continue to breed in the woods, but spotted flycatchers are now only intermittent nesters. Cuckoos and turtle doves are in serious decline too, though both can still be seen, or more likely heard, at Minsmere. Resident woodland birds which have now established territories and nests include marsh tits, coal tits, nuthatches, treecreepers, goldcrests, long-tailed tits and sparrowhawks.

On the heaths listen for singing Dartford warblers, stonechats, linnets, yellowhammers and woodlarks which can be seen from the network of public footpaths and bridleways. Passage migrants here might include whinchats, wheatears, tree pipits or red-backed shrikes.

Minsmere has contributed to the dramatic spread of Cetti's warblers into south-east England. From just a handful of pairs in 2000, they are now widespread around the scrubby wetland margins of all Suffolk's coastal nature reserves. These secretive birds are best detected by their explosive song of clear, penetrating notes that stops as abruptly as it begins.

Over the reedbed, male marsh harriers may be circling, diving and tumbling in their spectacular sky-dancing displays, or carrying sticks as nesting material in their talons. At Minsmere, each male regularly has more than one female and each female has her own nest. After falling to a single breeding pair at Minsmere in 1971 – the last pair in the UK – there are now about 14 nests annually, with a record 28 chicks reared in 2008.

In the reedbed, where the green stems of the newly growing reeds are growing upwards through the dry winter leaf litter, reed buntings are establishing their territories and the strident tones of sedge warblers may be heard. With luck you may hear the 'reeling' song of the increasingly rare grasshopper warbler.

Bearded tits are building their roofed nests low in the more dense areas, while the shy reed warblers construct their tightly woven, cup-shaped nests carefully bound to the reed stems, always under threat from the parasitic cuckoos arriving from late April onwards.

The arrival of swifts, to accompany the swallows and martins sweeping over the reedbeds in early May, signals the coming of summer. The season's influx is completed by the arrival of nightjars announcing their presence with long, churring calls in the late evenings on the heaths.

Among the earliest butterflies, look for orange tips flitting around wet meadows rich in cuckoo-flower, and green hairstreaks resting on gorse or tree lupin bushes along the dunes. The first dragonflies take to the wing as they emerge from their aquatic larval stage. Hairy dragonflies and large red damselflies may emerge in late April, followed by four-spotted and broad-bodied chasers and more of the commoner damselflies.

EARLY EMERGENCE: Four-spotted chaser is one of the first dragonflies to be seen on the wing.

FEEDING FOR THEMSELVES: Young avocets find their own food on the invertebrate-rich Scrape, while their ever-vigilant parents keep watch and attempt to keep predatory gulls at bay.

SUMMER: JUNE, JULY, AUGUST

As summer begins, the breeding season is well under way and the carefully managed habitats are being exploited by nesting birds.

On the Scrape, water levels are gradually lowered and by June the first fledgling gulls and terns appear on the mud and islands, surrounded by hundreds of diving, screaming adults.

Downy, brown and grey avocet chicks may be foraging along the edge of the Scrape, their aggressive parents attempting to keep the predatory gulls at bay. Brown-downed redshank and lapwing chicks also explore for food on the wet mud, their parents attracting attention by their anxious, chipping calls.

These young birds are extremely vulnerable, not only to predatory gulls and crows, but also to stoats, weasels and foxes. However, the Scrape's protective electric fencing keeps out most of the larger ground predators.

POPULAR SUBJECT: The swallows that nest at the Sluice often pose for the cameras and must be among the most photographed birds in the UK.

Family parties of mallards, gadwalls and shovelers may be seen criss-crossing the pools, the chicks being supervised by the females. The males stay separate in large groups and moult at this time.

From Bittern and Island Mere hides good opportunities arise for the patient observer. Young little and great crested grebes may hitch a lift on their parents' backs, while coot and moorhen parents oversee the hungry brood between them. Grey herons and little egrets fish along the reed edges and the shrill screams of water rails may be heard. Sometimes a pair of otters may break the surface or a swooping hobby may fly across in pursuit of a dragonfly.

Male and female marsh harriers can commonly be seen quartering the marshes, low over the reeds, or perching in one of the small trees dotted around the old field margins of the original farmland. During incubation, hunting is done by the males with the females progressively taking over once the young have hatched.

GOOD POPULATION: Gadwalls have built up in number over recent years at Minsmere.

From the hides there are frequent opportunities to watch the harriers' spectacular food passes in which the male passes food in mid-air to the female. In mid-June, the year's young marsh harriers, often known as 'flappers', make their first appearance above the reed tops.

Groups of bearded tits may be heard calling and, on still days, they may be seen searching the reeds for insects with which to feed their young. Reed and sedge warblers are busy feeding chicks and become less vocal, while even the usually noisy Cetti's warblers will stop singing for a few weeks while they moult after the stresses of breeding.

This is the best time to look for bitterns as females fly over the reeds and open water between their nests and their feeding sites. Patience is usually rewarded with a glimpse of a bittern on one of these feeding flights. They may also be seen searching for fish, stalking slowly and carefully through the water between the reeds.

On the paths leading to the hides, the purple spikes of southern marsh orchids flower abundantly, as do yellow irises. Along the path between West hide and Minsmere Sluice, look for the pale pink flowers and woolly leaves of marsh mallow, interspersed with clumps of great willowherb or hemp agrimony. Marsh sow-thistles add a splash of yellow as they tower above the reeds.

By late June, the woodland areas have become quieter as first the nightingales, then the warblers, complete their breeding and prepare to depart. Later on, fruiting elder and blackberry bushes in the North Bushes attract good numbers of warblers, especially whitethroats and lesser whitethroats as they refuel before migration.

The heath is at its best in mid-summer as the flowering heather turns the entire landscape purple. This is also the time to visit the heath at dusk in search of the elusive nightjar. Its mechanical 'churring' calls are easily heard on calm evenings and with luck you may catch a glimpse of one flitting between songposts. You may also catch sight of the luminous light of the glow worms coming from the low vegetation.

This is the best time to search for dragonflies. Even around the pond below the visitor centre, you should glimpse the imposing emperor dragonfly, brown, southern or migrant hawkers, and ruddy and common darters. Black-tailed skimmers may sit on the paths and emerald damselflies flit across reedbed pools. You may glimpse the jewel-like banded demoiselle along the New Cut, especially at Eastbridge.

Even at the height of the breeding season on the Suffolk coast, birds from further north begin to appear on their way south. As early as mid-June, groups of female spotted redshanks, still in dark summer plumage, gather on the Scrape, having stayed in their northern haunts just long enough to lay their eggs, leaving the males to rear the young.

July and August is a busy time for the wader-watcher. Up to 30 species may be observed. Some will over-winter here or in other parts of Britain. Others may rest and feed before moving on to warmer climates.

The most numerous species will be dunlin and black-tailed godwit. Search carefully among the dunlins and you may spot a few

EASY AND HARD: Little egret, main photo, is frequently seen around the reserve, but visitors often struggle to catch even the briefest glimpse of a nightingale, inset, as the species is often concealed by cover.

little stints, curlew sandpipers or knots, or maybe even a lost vagrant from Siberia or North America such as a pectoral or white-rumped sandpiper. Among the black-tailed godwits you may see a few ruffs, greenshanks and bar-tailed godwits, or maybe a whimbrel.

This is a good time of year to see flocks of little gulls on the Scrape. Flocks of common terns are joined by little and Sandwich terns and there may be a few Arctic, roseate or black terns.

Through July and August newly independent shelduck young gather in large groups on the Scrape. They are supervised by a few non-breeding adults while their parents migrate with thousands of others to moult off the German coast.

Little egret numbers peak at this time and it is also a good time for spoonbills. The Scrape is quieter by mid-August as the avocets and gulls move to other feeding grounds and the terns begin their migrations, but the duck numbers are building up with the arrival of teals, wigeons and pintails in their drab moult plumage.

SCARCE VAGRANT: Pectoral sandpiper is among the species of wader which call in to the reserve on their migratory travels.

During August, on cloudy nights with easterly winds, many nocturnal migrants, which navigate by the stars, may become disoriented and make landfall on this coast. Soon after dawn, bushes may contain flocks of common warblers, flycatchers and chats. Fortunate birdwatchers may find the occasional vagrant and drift migrant species such as icterine warbler, wryneck, or red-backed shrike.

HOVERING 'HUMMER': Hummingbird hawkmoth is an occasional visitor to the buddleia bushes around the reserve centre.

WELL-NAMED: The dramatic wasp spider recalls the insect which gives it its name and little gull, inset, is the smallest in its family.

Offshore, seawatching becomes more productive. Fulmars, Arctic skuas, common scoters, gannets and little gulls are all regularly seen and the potential for such exciting species as sooty shearwater and long-tailed skua increases, especially in periods of strong, onshore winds.

Throughout the summer, flowering plants such as the widespread marsh mallow provide nectar for butterflies and moths. Buddleia bushes near the visitor centre attract clouds of butterflies, including migrant painted ladies and ragged-edged commas.

Occasionally a few hummingbird hawkmoths may also be present too.

In the woods, look for white admirals feeding on bramble flowers or for purple hairstreaks flying high in the oak canopy. Around the short grass look for ringlets, meadow browns, graylings, small coppers, brown argus, and skippers.

In late summer, search carefully among the long grass near the Sluice and you might find a wasp spider resting on her web. She is well-named as she sports black, brown and yellow stripes.

Reserve reflections: a special day in Minsmere's history

Photos: JON EVANS

The Fall

'At times, in the correct weather conditions, a 'fall' of migrants may occur. Indeed, Britain's biggest recorded deluge of birds took place here on September 3 1965, when a deep depression over Europe caused a 'fall' of some 400,000 disorientated and exhausted birds to arrive on a small stretch of the Suffolk coast. From Lowestoft south to Minsmere huge numbers of Scandinavian migrants were grounded by a combination of torrential rain and onshore winds. On the reserve, a total of 200,000 small birds of 52 species arrived overnight and throughout the morning. They included wheatears, redstarts, garden warblers, pied flycatchers, bluethroats, wrynecks, icterine warblers, red-backed shrikes and ortolan buntings. Such a 'fall' is unlikely to be witnessed again. I wish I'd been there!'

John Grant, Minsmere Volunteer

HISTORIC DAY: Wrynecks, main photo, redstarts, above left, and red-backed shrikes, above right, were among the species involved in the mass arrival of migrants to Minsmere on September 3 1965.

AUTUMN: SEPTEMBER, OCTOBER, NOVEMBER

This is the season when millions of birds move south throughout Europe from their summer breeding grounds. Many have left areas well inside the Arctic Circle, where in June, July and early August there is plentiful food and unbroken daylight in which to find it. But as the short northern summer comes to an end, it is time to head south.

Many birds migrate across the Continent and only arrive on the Suffolk coast if blown off course by easterly winds, giving observers on this coast a chance to see some rare and unusual birds. This visible migration can be an awe-inspiring spectacle. Often, around sunrise, small flocks of birds may be heard calling as they pass through – wagtails, finches, pipits and skylarks.

The offshore movement of ducks, geese and seabirds continues. Diligent observers sometimes pick out Arctic and black terns on the move and the first big numbers of brent geese may be logged. Suffolk's first king eider lingered for several weeks in 2010.

A clear, still day in September is a perfect time to search along the seasonal trail through the reedbed. Here, you may hear the 'pinging' calls from family groups of bearded tits as they erupt out of the reeds, where they are feeding on fallen seeds and seed-heads.

By October and November, fieldfares and redwings have arrived from Scandinavia, accompanied by Continental blackbirds, song thrushes, bramblings and goldcrests. These will be seen throughout the winter months but Asiatic species such as Pallas's warbler, yellow-browed warbler or red-flanked bluetail, which can set the pulses racing at this time, are more transient.

An impressive array of vagrants has been recorded on the reserve at this time of year, among them the UK's first Siberian blue robin. If that can turn up it could be said that almost anything can.

Wildfowl numbers increase on the pools, grazing marshes and the Scrape. Large flocks of wigeons and teals can be seen and the first white-fronted geese, Bewick's swans and whooper swans arrive from late October, often in family groups, to settle in for the winter. This is a good time to see otters from Island Mere hide.

One of the most spectacular displays in the natural world is the swirling clouds of starlings gathering at dusk before dropping down into a coastal reedbed to roost. Such flocks can be seen at Minsmere at some point in most winters, but their occurrence is unpredictable so please contact the reserve for the latest news.

In September and October, during the rutting season, the Minsmere herd of red deer is at its most visible and dramatic. Groups of hinds gather on the heath and can be seen from the RSPB viewing point, as the stags bellow and fight to win their favours. The action peaks in early morning and again in the evening, when the bellowing calls of the stags sound quite eerie and evocative of times past.

This spectacle is one of Minsmere's star attractions. A viewpoint is usually signed from the car park on the Westleton-Dunwich road. As well as the deer, you may see stone-curlews, green woodpeckers, little owls and foxes from here.

SPECTACULAR DISPLAY: Swirling clouds of starlings gathering at dusk are a stirring sight on winter afternoons at Minsmere.

MIGRANT AND RESIDENT: Brambling, right, is a visitor from the north, but Cetti's warbler, above, is a permanent feature of Minsmere's reedbed edges.

WELCOME: The new visitor centre at RSPB Minsmere offers first class facilities including a shop and café.

RESERVE INFORMATION

Opening Times

Car park, nature trails and hides are open daily, except 25 and 26 December, from dawn to dusk.
Visitor centre, café and shop are open daily, except 25 and 26 December, from 9 am to 5 pm.
The visitor centre closes at 4 pm from 1 November to 31 January.
Discovery Centre opening times vary, depending on bookings.
Several miles of public rights of way around the reserve are open at all times and parts of the heath are designated as open access land.

How to get there

Follow the brown tourist signs from the A12 at Blythburgh (coming from the north), or Yoxford (from south and west) via Westleton village.
By public transport, the nearest rain station is at Darsham and buses run to Leiston or Saxmundham. From there, use Suffolk Link Blyth, a demand-responsive bus service (call 01728 833526 to book).

Cost

Free to members
Non-members Adults: £7.50
Non-members Children: £3.00
Concessionary: £5.00
Family Ticket: (Up to two adults and four children): £15.00. (Prices as at June 2012)

Facilities

- Visitor centre with welcome area, RSPB shop and café and fully accessible toilets.
- Two circular walks each about 1.5 miles (2.4 km) long, with information boards. Parts of these walks are not accessible for wheelchairs.
- Eight hides and viewpoints, four of which are wheelchair accessible.
- Discovery Centre and Wild Zone for family fun and field teacher-led education programmes.
- A programme of guided walk, demonstrations, workshops and family activities.

Further Information

Contact: RSPB Minsmere, Westleton, Saxmundham, Suffolk IP17 3BY, tel: 01728 648281; email: minsmere@rspb.org.uk or see www.rspb.org.uk/minsmere

DISCOVERING NATURE: The pond in the reserve's former main car park is proving popular with children, and the new Wild Zone, below, left and above, near the Discovery Centre, offers wildlife play opportunities.

North Warren & Aldringham Walks

A lacework of peaceful paths

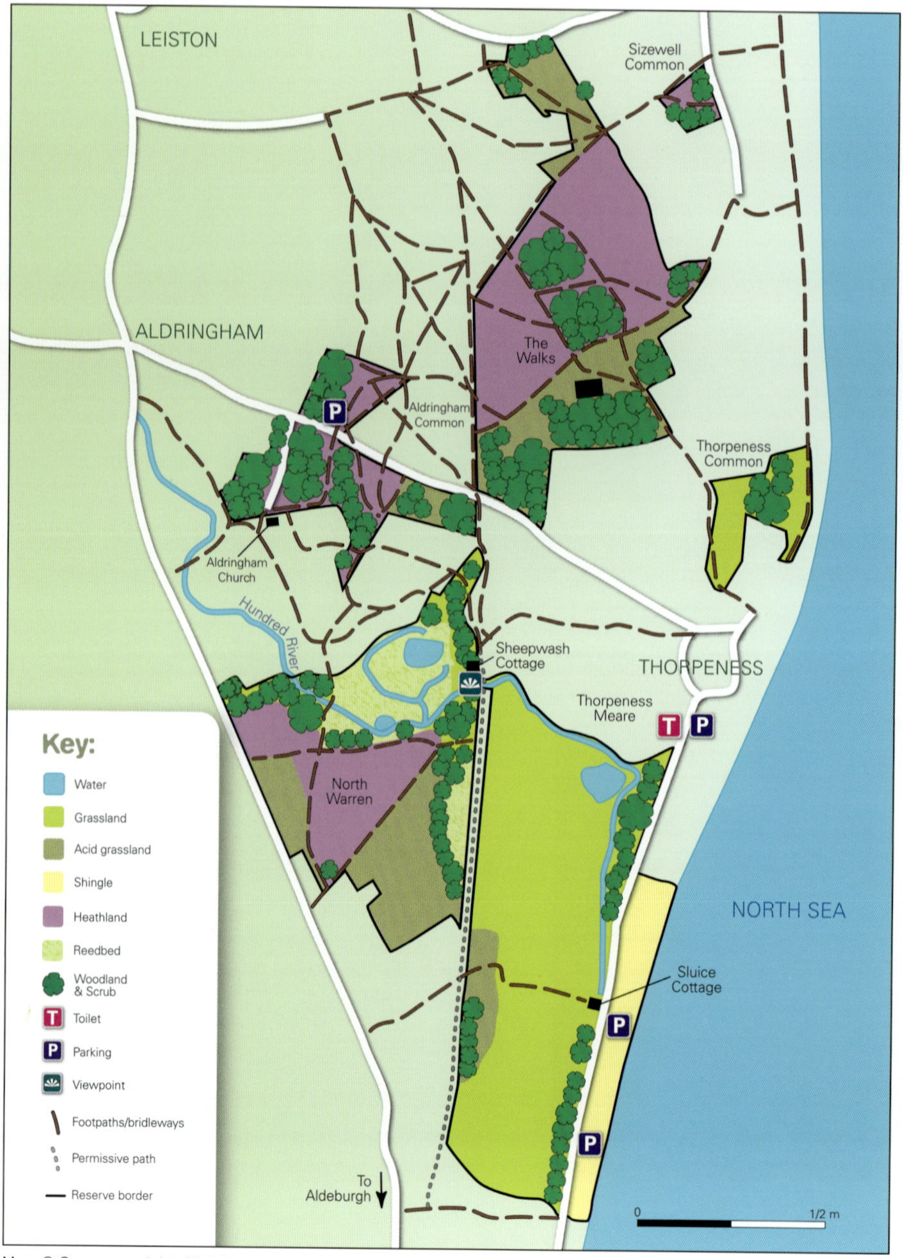

IN FROM THE NORTH:
The grazing marshes at North Warren have become an important wintering site for Eurasian white-fronted geese, inset.

Main photo: IAN BARTHORPE

Geography and history

North Warren, between Thorpeness and Aldeburgh, was one of the first RSPB reserves. The wetland heart of the reserve is in the valley of the Hundred River. The mudflats of the original estuary were used in 1912 to create Thorpeness Meare, a shallow boating lake, for the developing Thorpeness holiday village. The lagoons and marshes, shown on 18th-Century maps as covering the present area of grazing marshes between Thorpeness and Aldeburgh, were also drained at this time.

The land was purchased by the RSPB in 1939, as a result of interest by local naturalists. The original reserve of 37 hectares (ha) was part of an area already well-known nationally for its interesting breeding birds – among them stone-curlews, bearded tits, Montagu's harriers, garganeys and bitterns.

More land has been acquired over the years and the present reserve covers an area of 443ha. This includes the heathland of Aldringham Walks to the north of Thorpeness, the area inland from Thorpeness Meare around the Hundred River, consisting of marsh, reedbed and fen, plus an area of mixed woodland and heathland running south to Aldeburgh.

Church Farm grazing marshes, east of the old railway line, were purchased in 1990 and the shingle ridge and foreshore from Haven House to Aldeburgh has also been acquired. Much of the reserve is accessible from a network of public footpaths.

Before the Second World War, a system of summer wardens or 'watchers' was introduced. The first was retired policeman Percy Cole, whose 1938 diary records his encounters with trespassers, rabbit-catchers, boys fishing, stray canoeists from The Meare and egg collectors. He recorded the annual breeding of Montagu's harriers – then, as now, a rare and exciting bird.

The reserve has had its difficult times. During the Second World War, the Army built pillboxes and trenches on the heath and wide tank traps across the marshes as part of the coastal defences.

The heathland areas had been kept closely grazed by sheep until the 1930s and after that by rabbits. Following the severe reduction in rabbit numbers from 1953 due to myxomatosis, these heaths became overgrown with bracken and scrub which submerged the heather and grasses. The once-familiar stone-curlew, whinchat and red-backed shrike ceased to breed.

Improved drainage of the marshes had its effect on the wetland areas of mere and reedbeds, where thatching reeds had been harvested until the 1950s. They were drying out and being invaded by willow scrub. As a result, many of the exciting birds for which the reserve had been acquired, such as bitterns, marsh harriers and bearded tits, were no longer in residence.

Until the railway line's closure in 1964, the steam trains running between Aldeburgh and Thorpeness caused frequent heath and reedbed fires. A particularly damaging one in 1954 destroyed 70ha of heather.

The present rich and varied appearance of the reserve, with its flourishing habitats and about 86 breeding bird species, dates from the 1990s. It is the product of years of visionary effort by the wardening team and a large band of volunteers, many of them from the RSPB Woodbridge Local Group.

Large areas of heather and acid grassland are in good condition, with much invasive scrub removed. These areas support nesting nightjars, Dartford warblers and woodlarks as well as a colony of silver-studded blue butterflies.

The reedbed has been rescued and the first bitterns since 1946 have successfully re-colonised the area. The marshes have been returned to traditional management to attract wintering geese and ducks and breeding and migrant waders. Looking ahead, due to the topography of the site, the reedbed should provide a safe haven for bitterns and other reedbed birds displaced by marine incursions elsewhere.

North Warren is now a very special place, much loved by those who can visit it often and discover its secrets throughout the year.

The reserve is deliberately planned as a quiet retreat, attractive to those who wish to walk the many paths through the heathland, marsh and woodland to view the wildlife and birds. It is accessible on public footpaths at all times.

Photo: MIKE PAGE

PEACEFUL PATHS: Aldringham Walks' heathland is easily accessible by a network of tracks.

WALK WITH HISTORY: The reserve footpath that follows the route of the old railway line. Inset, Aldringham Walks is the heathland home of specialist species such as nightjar, top left, and woodlark, top right.

Habitats and management

The reserve is part of the complex of wetland and heathland habitats of the Suffolk Coast & Heaths Area of Outstanding Natural Beauty and is within the area designated as Suffolk's Heritage Coast. It is managed under Higher Level Stewardship and Environmentally Sensitive Area agreements, both of which are Government agri-environment grant schemes. Its quality is demonstrated by its designation as a Site of Special Scientific Interest and parts of the reserve are within a designated Special Protection Area.

The heathland soils are mainly glacial sands and gravels, the marshes are on alluvium and clay, the fens and reedbed on a layer of peat and the reserve is bordered by a shingle beach. Consequently, the reserve contains a diverse mosaic of habitats with areas of reedbed, lowland wet grassland, lowland heath and vegetated shingle ridge.

The lowland heath is one of the largest remnants of the once extensive Suffolk Sandlings.

THRIVING: Dartford warblers have returned to the Suffolk Sandlings and now thrive on the reserve.

In 1990 the first full-time warden, Rob Macklin, set out to recreate the pristine environments of the pre-war years. His extensive knowledge of wildlife, combined with his skills in organising drainage, sluices, mechanical diggers and a host of scrub-clearing volunteers, enabled him to reverse the decline in these valuable wetland and heathland habitats.

Sandlings heath

The vision guiding the heathland management at North Warren and Aldringham Walks has been the restoration of breeding woodlarks and the establishment of silver-studded blue butterflies, relocated from Westleton Heath. Both flourish in warm, well-drained locations and low-growing grass and heather. Once widespread, the woodlark declined to only a few pairs on the Suffolk coast by the 1980s, but attempts since then to increase its numbers have been only partially successful.

CAREFUL MANAGEMENT: Some trees are left standing to bring diversity to the heathlands.

Management work also successfully targeted nightjars, an elusive nocturnal bird preferring woodland margins on the heaths. Dartford warblers have also re-colonised the area. After an absence from Suffolk of more than 50 years, this species returned to the county in the late 1990s and soon began to nest at Aldringham Walks.

The restoration of the acid grass and heather has been a major task, involving the removal of swathes of invasive silver birch and pine scrub. Some has been cleared with machinery, but much of it has been taken out by hand by local volunteers on their monthly working parties. The suffocating bracken has had to be tackled by cutting and treatment with a selective herbicide. Accidental burning such as the 2009 fire, which destroyed 4ha of gorse and heather, can be beneficial, as it encourages regeneration.

The heather is flourishing in the north of the reserve and can now be managed by cutting a small area each year on a 20-year rotation to provide a variety of vegetation heights. Visitors in the summer can admire the wide stretches of purple heather or ling.

Gorse is a valuable wildlife habitat – whitethroats, linnets and yellowhammers breed in the thickets and Dartford warblers

ACCESS POINT: A footpath sign guides visitors across the marshes from the Aldeburgh-Thorpeness road near the derelict property known as Sluice Cottage.

can be seen singing from the tops of the bushes. However, the gorse needs careful control by coppicing, which is done in a 10-12 year rotation.

Rabbits have been a mixed blessing on the reserve. They maintain the short sward of acid grass but sometimes need to be excluded with electric fencing from the areas of young, newly growing heather. In addition to mowing, the traditional management for grassland is grazing by animals. So now Exmoor and Dartmoor ponies graze the coarse vegetation at North Warren and Aldringham Walks, keeping the acid grassland sward in perfect shape.

Grazing marshes

The purchase in 1990 of Church Farm Marshes, the 98ha of land between the old railway line and the sea, began to reverse the decline of this area. The marshes had been drained and so were too dry for wintering or breeding birds. Traditional management methods returned – and so did the birds.

Increasing the water levels in winter by sluice adjustment creates areas of shallow flooding on the grassland which are attractive to wintering and migrating wildfowl and waders. The water levels in the northern marsh can be separately controlled so that they are kept wetter for longer during the spring to encourage waders to feed and then to nest.

The return of flocks of white-fronted geese and wigeons has been a triumph of habitat management and a spectacular sight for birdwatchers. Lapwings, teals and dunlins are just some of the birds which take advantage of the undisturbed feeding and roosting sites in these wet meadows. Teals in particular feed extensively on seeds of saltmarsh rush when these areas are shallow-flooded. Waders with probing beaks search out earthworms and other soil invertebrates in the soft, damp ground.

Konik ponies graze the wetter areas during winter to ensure that the grass is kept short for the start of the breeding season and these are replaced in spring by cattle. In some of the higher, drier fields where skylarks nest, the grazing is delayed until mid-summer. Some hay may be cut after the breeding of ground-nesting birds is

North Warren & Aldringham Walks

complete. Rushes and thistles are cut mechanically in the autumn, but some vegetation is left longer to provide cover for breeding redshanks in the following spring.

Dykes are cleaned out in rotation but important reed cover for breeding warblers is retained. The plentiful supply of slow-moving fresh water provides the ideal conditions for water voles and breeding dragonflies and damselflies.

Main photo: JENNY JAMES, inset, JON EVANS

MANAGEMENT SUCCESS: Significant numbers of Eurasian white-fronted geese, right, make use of the reserve's wet grassland, main photo, each winter.

As a result of these traditional farming techniques, the marshes usually support around 20 successful breeding pairs each of lapwings and redshanks and the remarkable total of 100 pairs of skylarks.

Reedbed

The area of reedbed in the Hundred River valley survived until the 1950s when further drainage dried it out allowing willow and alder scrub to invade and the former rich variety of breeding birds was lost.

Main photo: IAN BARTHORPE, inset, JON EVANS

REEDBED REWARDS: Management work has enhanced the reedbeds for specialist species such as bittern, inset.

A major project has lowered the level by 30cm and felled the invasive trees, providing an extensive new habitat of wet reedbed. Internal ditches and some deeper pools are important in dry summers for maintaining the populations of small freshwater fish such as roach, rudd and tench which are food for the young bitterns. The reedbed is managed both by hand and by using an amphibious reed-cutting machine, a Truxor, which cuts and collects the reeds.

The reward has been increasing numbers of breeding reedbed birds. The return of bearded tits, marsh harriers, water rails and finally, in 2000, bitterns, has been accompanied by a striking increase in the numbers of Cetti's, sedge and reed warblers. An additional welcome return is that of otters, now confirmed as residents on the reserve.

The vegetation in the reserve's fen habitats is cut and burned in rotation in late summer to encourage the growth of typical colourful wetland flowering plants such as ragged robin, purple loosestrife and southern marsh orchid. An important colony of the less-colourful adder's tongue fern can also be found here.

Walkers on the reedbed boardwalk can appreciate these restored habitats as they hear the 'pinging' calls of bearded tits or see a marsh harrier quartering over the reeds as groups of hobbies swoop after dragonflies from spring until late summer. Common lizards can also be seen basking on the boardwalk.

Woodland

Although the reserve is chiefly important for heaths and wetlands, there are over 100ha of mixed woodland and scrub which provide a superb habitat for a wide range of songbirds such as nightingales and various warblers, finches and buntings.

Some of the alder and oak woodland around the Hundred River has been left untouched, with dead trees left in place for great spotted woodpeckers to drill for insect larvae in the rotting wood. Nestboxes that have attracted 170 pairs each of blue tits and great tits can be observed in many parts of the woodland, only a few feet from the ground for easy monitoring of the eggs and young.

The alder carr in the wetter parts of the woodland is an important breeding place for the attractive, but increasingly scarce, marsh tit. The alder cones also provide winter food for seed-eating birds

The importance of scrub in woodland clearings and along the old railway line cannot be overstated. Increasingly damaged by feeding muntjac deer, these areas are an important nightingale habitat. Early morning in early summer is the best time to appreciate them and the other songbirds that flourish here.

WOODLAND RESIDENT: Great spotted woodpeckers are often seen in the woods

Photo: TOM MARSHALL (rspb-images.com)

North Warren & Aldringham Walks

HERE BE DRAGONS: North Warren is home to a wealth of dragonfly and damselfly species, including migrant hawker, main photo, ruddy darter, inset left, and blue-tailed damselfly, inset right.

Foreshore

The shingle ridge, now dominated at the southern end by the Benjamin Britten memorial sculpture – 'Scallop' – is part of the reserve and has unlimited public access. Management of this fragile and interesting habitat needs to protect the nationally scarce specialist plants associated with shingle. In summer, some areas are temporarily fenced off to protect the fragile sea pea. Look out for the sand catchfly, a rare sand dune plant of disturbed ground.

LOCAL LANDMARK: The sculpture 'Scallop' stands on the beach where snow buntings, inset, can often be seen on winter days.

PASTORAL SCENE: Imposing pine trees form an impressive backdrop as cattle graze on the reserve.

Fauna

The mammals most likely to be seen are rabbits. They are predated by foxes, but with minimal impact on their numbers. There are also badgers on the reserve. Water voles, which flourish in the pools and ditches, are vulnerable to predation by stoats but there are few, if any, mink to deplete their numbers. They are not under threat from the otters here.

FLOURISHING BUT VULNERABLE: Water voles can be seen but sometimes fall prey to stoats.

Red deer and muntjac occur in small numbers and can be seen at any time of day. Wood and harvest mice, and water, common and pygmy shrews are a good source of food for the reserve's wide variety of resident and migrant raptors. A colony of pipistrelle bats roosts in the north of the reserve and can be seen flying at dusk over Aldringham Walks.

On the light, easily warmed sandy soils of the heaths, adders, slow worms and common lizards are most likely to be seen on sunny days. Grass snakes are flourishing and abundant in many parts of the reserve, especially in the reed bundles left on the reedbed edges after cutting. The warm conditions of rotting vegetation are ideal for the developing eggs and young. The wetlands provide suitable locations for common frogs and toads and smooth and palmate newts.

The old railway line, a permissive footpath through the reserve, is a great place to see butterflies. Thirty-five species are listed for the reserve in local records kept since 1900. There is a mixture of woodland species, including the familiar red admiral and peacock, and species more common on the open sandy heath, such as grayling and small copper.

In May, green hairstreaks can be seen over the extensive gorse patches in several parts of the heath. In late summer, around the tops of the oak trees, the fluttering flight of the purple hairstreak is unmistakable.

The special butterfly of this reserve, however, is the silver-studded blue. This species was introduced to Aldringham Walks in 1999 with individuals from Westleton Heath and has established a successful colony. Numbers vary annually with up to 150 adults seen in the better years.

SANDY SOILS: The declining grayling butterfly can still be found on the reserve's open heathland areas.

Although less obvious, 260 species of moth have been recorded on the reserve. They include some rarities such as the white-mantled wainscot, ground lackey and marbled clover.

The old railway line is also an exceptional site for dragonflies. Hairy dragonflies are followed by brown and southern hawkers in high summer as they hatch from nearby pools and ditches. The migrant hawker appears here in substantial numbers and the Norfolk hawker has begun to breed here for the first time.

Common and ruddy darter dragonflies may be seen from the path across the grazing marshes. Red-veined darters, blue-tailed damselflies and the recently established small red-eyed damselfly may be seen over stretches of water.

Crickets and grasshoppers are common all over the reserve, especially on the edges of the grazing marshes. The huge size of the great green bush cricket and the noisy buzz of Röesel's bush cricket are both impressive.

Glow worms can be seen at dusk on the heaths and antlions – a type of lacewing – occur on south-facing sandy banks on the heath and cliffs at Aldringham Walks. There can be up to 2,000 of the larval pits in which the antlion larvae lurk for their prey and this represents a significant proportion of the UK population.

Flora

Each part of the reserve has a range of characteristic plant species which dominate their area but, among these, smaller numbers of other colourful plants – some rare or unusual – flower through the seasons. Some areas of heath are dominated by ling heather, interspersed with smaller patches of bright purple bell heather.

However, much of the heathland vegetation is acid grasses, mainly fescues, interspersed in some places with the tall blue spikes of viper's bugloss. Common ragwort, which also grows freely, is allowed

ON THE BEACH: Sea pea can be seen in extensive patches on the shingle ridge.

SPLASHES OF COLOUR: The yellow horned-poppy brightens up the reserve's shingle ridge, and bee orchid, inset, is a species that can be found on the drier, sandy areas in parts of the reserve.

to flower as a source of nectar for a range of insects, especially bees and butterflies. However, it is cut before seeding to prevent it spreading.

In high summer, the numerous butterflies along the old railway line take advantage of the nectar of flowering hemp agrimony. Around the edges of the reeds in the fen, bogbean, ragged robin, yellow iris, southern marsh orchids, meadowsweet and purple loosestrife flower in sequence from late spring to high summer and the yellow flowers of the rare marsh sow-thistle rise between the reeds with the heads of the reedmace.

In the maze of drainage ditches through the marshes, greater and lesser spearwort and a rare brackish water crowfoot are among the aquatic plants to be seen. In summer the pink sea pea flowers in extensive patches on the shingle ridge together with the yellow horned-poppy and the increasingly rare sea kale. Bee orchids may sometimes be seen in the sandy areas.

Wildlife season by season

WINTER: DECEMBER, JANUARY, FEBRUARY

The arrival of the wintering wildfowl is the highlight of the birdwatching year for many of North Warren's frequent visitors. The view of the grazing marshes from the coast road car park or from the tracks across the marshes is best in the morning, with the low winter sun behind you – and the east wind on your back. Another good viewpoint is the old railway line. It is also best when it is high tide on the nearby River Alde as estuarine birds will then fly onto the reserve's fields.

The arrival of flocks up to 3,000 wigeons, together with 1,500 lapwings and 1,000 teals can be a spectacular sight. However, it is the geese that are the main attraction.

This is the best site in Suffolk to see large numbers of white-fronted geese at close quarters; numbers reached a remarkable 850 in January 2011. In addition, feral

HANDSOME VISITOR: Flocks of fieldfares may be around the reserve, exploiting any remaining berries.

barnacle, greylag and Canada geese are readily seen.

The reserve's speciality at this time of year, however, is the petite tundra bean goose. North Warren has become one of the most reliable sites in the UK for this attractive species. Small numbers may often be seen grazing in the wet pastures at the northern end of the grazing marshes, although they can sometimes be lost to view for long periods in the undulations of the land.

Good numbers of gadwalls, mallards, pintails and shovelers will almost certainly be more easily seen. Redshanks, black-tailed godwits, curlews and common snipe may be searching the mud for worms and insects. Look out here for occasional small numbers of wintering water pipits.

From the shingle ridge, sea-watchers can scan the waves for part of the Sole Bay flock of up to 4,000 red-throated divers. Among these may be some of the bay's 700 or so wintering great crested grebes and passing eiders, scoters, guillemots and razorbills may also be seen. Small flocks of snow buntings occasionally visit the beach to feed among the patches of sparse shingle vegetation.

The reedbed is best viewed at this time from the viewpoint near Sheepwash Cottage on the old railway line. At dusk, 30,000 starlings may arrive here in swirling clouds – a sight and sound to remember. They roost in the reedbeds here or elsewhere on the Suffolk coast. Dusk also brings several marsh harriers to roost in the reedbed.

From the paths through the woodland, flocks of siskins, redpolls and goldfinches may be seen feeding in the alders and any remaining hawthorn or holly berries may be exploited by redwings or fieldfares.

The first signs of spring can be detected in February when, on warm, sunny days, Dartford warblers may be calling on the heaths and woodlarks may be song-flighting overhead. Skylarks will sing over the grazing marshes as the geese, ducks and waders begin to depart on their long migrations north to their summer breeding grounds. In the reedbed, male bitterns will begin booming to claim their territories and attract the females.

Spring: March, April, May

As the winter migrants depart from the grazing marshes, passage migrants temporarily take their place. Passage waders build up from March, when black-tailed godwits are often the forerunners of species such as whimbrel, greenshank, turnstone and ringed plover.

In April and May the grazing marsh often attracts spoonbills and in recent years a single great white egret has joined the resident little egrets on the reserve. Gadwalls may begin to nest and this is a good time to observe bitterns and marsh harriers as they establish their territories. Very occasionally, spring rarities such as bee-eaters and hoopoes cause a pulse of excitement.

This is a time of year when observers are well advised to keep their eyes on the skies as the reserve has notched up an impressive array of passage raptors.

On warm, sunny mornings birds of prey often pass over as they head north. Ospreys, common buzzards and red kites can be reliably predicted but rough-legged buzzards, and – later in spring – honey buzzards, black kites, red-footed falcons and Montagu's harriers are more unusual.

In the woodland and on the heaths summer migrants arrive from April onwards and, together with resident species, begin to establish their breeding territories. The first to arrive are the chiffchaffs. Later, the reserve's population of 200 pairs of common whitethroats and 30 pairs of lesser whitethroats builds up. Blackcaps and garden warblers contribute their songs together with the resident blackbirds and song and mistle thrushes.

Nightingales take advantage of the many patches of bramble and low scrub on Aldringham Walks to build their well-concealed nests. On the heath at Aldringham Walks, nightjars return and males may be heard 'churring' at dusk.

Listen for the lilting song of the woodlark. Still scarce birds, woodlarks struggle with the cold winters and, as ground-nesting birds, they are especially vulnerable to disturbance from dogs and predation by foxes and carrion crows.

On the grazing marshes, lapwings take up their territories on the well-grazed grassland, driving off their rivals with spectacular dives and distinctive calls. When their nests are established they are always on the look-out for predators. Redshanks choose the rougher pasture, laying their eggs in a shallow scrape protected by tussocky vegetation. Over the higher, drier fields the continuous songs of skylarks fill the air as they prepare to raise their young.

Hobbies will be swooping and feeding on the plentiful supply of insects. Among the reeds, heard perhaps but not often seen, bearded tits and reed, sedge, grasshopper and Cetti's warblers will be nesting and feeding their young. In the early morning, the shrill squeal of the water rails will contribute to the dawn chorus.

Photo: LOWESTOFT LOUNGE LIZARDS

Photo: LOWESTOFT LOUNGE LIZARDS

HEALTHY POPULATIONS: North Warren & Aldringham Walks support impressive numbers of breeding common whitethroats, and lesser whitethroats, left.

DASHING PREDATOR: Hobbies often hunt for dragonflies which are caught on the wing.

Summer: June, July, August

As the summer progresses, the reserve becomes quieter. The nightingales, and then the other songbirds, cease their territorial singing and their young fledge from the nests. At this time families of young birds such as linnets and yellowhammers can be seen moving through the yellow flowering gorse on the heaths.

In the fen, on still mornings, where the spikes of purple loosestrife punctuate the deepening green of the reed heads, groups of bearded tits call as they search for seeds and insects.

The breeding success of the reserve's bitterns, nesting here again since 2000, can be assessed during these months. Although males have finished booming, during the day females can be glimpsed as they return to the nests carrying food for the young.

Marsh harriers also have returned to the reserve and up to four pairs have bred annually since 2000. Males and females can be seen over the marshes or quartering and displaying over the reedbed. They have been observed attacking bitterns and magpies attempting to take young from their nests or they may themselves be mobbed by carrion crows. By July juveniles will be out over the reeds, both parents flying with their young and passing food to them in mid-air.

The emerging adult dragonflies attract groups of up to 20 hobbies which can be seen swooping low over the reeds to capture them.

On the marshes, the calls and displays of the lapwing and redshank parents distract potential predators from their young as they cower in the lengthening grass and rushes. Walk along the shingle ridge now, to see the sea pea and the yellow horned-poppy in flower. Warm, still summer evenings are the time to choose for visiting Aldringham Walks to hear and see the nightjars in their favourite territory as they hunt for moths at dusk.

The first autumn migrants appear on the reserve in July and August. These will be breeding birds from as far north as the Arctic following the coast on their route south. In the beach scrub, especially north of Thorpeness, smaller birds such as redstarts and pied flycatchers can be seen resting while the first flocks of curlews arrive to feed on the grazing marshes, with the occasional green sandpiper alongside. The spectacular black-tailed godwits will be in flocks on the marshes from as early as June, their dramatic plumage revealed as they fly up when disturbed.

Autumn: September, October, November

The autumn passage continues with redstarts and pied flycatchers passing through, and icterine and barred warblers occasionally being noted in periods of easterly winds in early September. The occasional arrival of a rare autumn passage migrant such as a red-flanked bluetail or a dusky warbler – again often associated with easterly winds, but later in the season – will attract a great deal of attention.

Out to sea, sooty and Manx shearwaters may be seen, but more common are gannets and little gulls which sometimes pass in impressive numbers. Skuas can be represented at this time with Arctic, pomarine, and great being fairly regular and long-tailed putting in less frequent appearances.

On the grazing meadows, small numbers of ruff may be seen among other passage wading species such as common sandpiper, greenshank and dunlin. The first groups of wigeons and teals arrive in September; their numbers increasing month by month through the autumn until the huge winter feeding flocks have assembled.

As the weather turns colder, more winter visitors arrive and by late October the first white-fronted geese may be heard calling as they fly over in straggling lines and descend to make their landfall from northern Russia. Depending on water levels, by the end of November there may be several thousand wildfowl feeding on the marshes, exploiting the plentiful food supplies in this enriched and restored environment.

BRIEF STOPOVER: Dunlins are among the many wading birds which stop by on the grazing marshes to refuel on their long journey south to their wintering areas.

RARE VISITOR: Red-flanked bluetails have become annual vagrants to Britain, and the species has been recorded at Aldringham Walks. They may be increasing but they still give birdwatchers a buzz of excitement.

Reserve reflections: special memories of North Warren

Memories of the Monty's, 1955

Stuart Keith was warden of North Warren in 1955 and had the privilege of watching breeding Montagu's harriers on his 'patch'. Perhaps one day the reserve will again host these rare, elegant raptors. We can but hope – until then we can enjoy the spectacle in words. Stuart takes up the tale....

❛ From June 27th I had established the locality in which we might expect to find the female bird sitting. Although the male would roam far afield from time to time, and sometimes for an hour or more, the female rose into the air only occasionally and for very short spells. On the return of the male after one of his roaming flights he always returned to the same spot, which was a fairly large tract of dried reeds quite close to the railway line from Aldeburgh to Thorpeness. Neither bird paid any attention to the passing trains at any time during the summer.

On several occasions I saw the female rise on the return of the male for an aerial pass of food from one to the other. On each occasion she went back to the reedbed.

Photo: BILL BASTON

It was about this period that I definitely established beyond doubt that there were two females and that the male was serving both. The second female was using a nesting site about 150 yards from the other. Although on one occasion I did see the three birds in the air at the same time it was very seldom that both females left the ground together.

There were occasions when the male would take to the upper air and give as fine a display of soaring as I have seen. The bird would drift in wide sweeps, then in circles, rising all the while to a great altitude.

Coming to rest from the air the harriers seldom if ever used the taller trees that grow round the sanctuary, preferring the thorn bushes, dead elders or sallows. More often they favoured an old fence post which would also be used for stripping. I often saw a female visit the stripping post of her mate after he had used it and on most occasions she was able to find some discarded morsel lying at the foot of the post. Whether this was done intentionally by the male I know not, but it happened frequently.

It is difficult to say exactly when the eggs were hatched. It was about the middle of August that I first heard the male calling. The nesting area being approached, he would call very rapidly:- 'Chi--ki,ki,ki,' and this repeated very frequently. It was a very high-pitched call. It would also be used – rather more slowly – on his return from hunting to bring up the female or, latterly, when there were young, to inform them that he was about to drop some food. The female too used this form of feeding her young and I began to believe the young birds had left the nest and were moving gradually out of the reedbed towards the grassland to the south. During the last days of August I observed four young harriers with a female on the ground with them.

The male at this time flew above with his warning call being repeated with obvious agitation. The young birds soon took to cover in the long, dense grasses. When they were safely hidden the female took wing and both parents flew off to a distance. The young birds looked fit and well. It was not until the end of the month that I saw them on the wing. ❜

QUIET CORNER: An impressive range of common and scarce dragonfly species can be seen at North Warren, particularly on summer days around the reserve's numerous wetland areas.

RESERVE INFORMATION

Opening times

Access at all times from public footpaths only.

How to get there

From the A12 via Aldeburgh or Leiston. Entrances and car parks on the beach road just north of Aldeburgh, in Thorpeness and on the Aldringham-Thorpeness road.

Facilities

- A network of public footpaths criss-crosses the reserve. See the information boards or pick up a reserve leaflet for recommended routes.
- Information boards in the public car parks at Aldeburgh and Thorpeness.
- Toilets at Thorpeness and Aldeburgh.
- Refreshments in Thorpeness and Aldeburgh.
- Wheelchair access on the beach only.

Further Information

Contact: The Warden, North Warren Nature Reserve, tel:01728 648780; email: minsmere@rspb.org.uk or see www.rspb.org.uk/northwarren

Snape Reserve

Creating new habitats

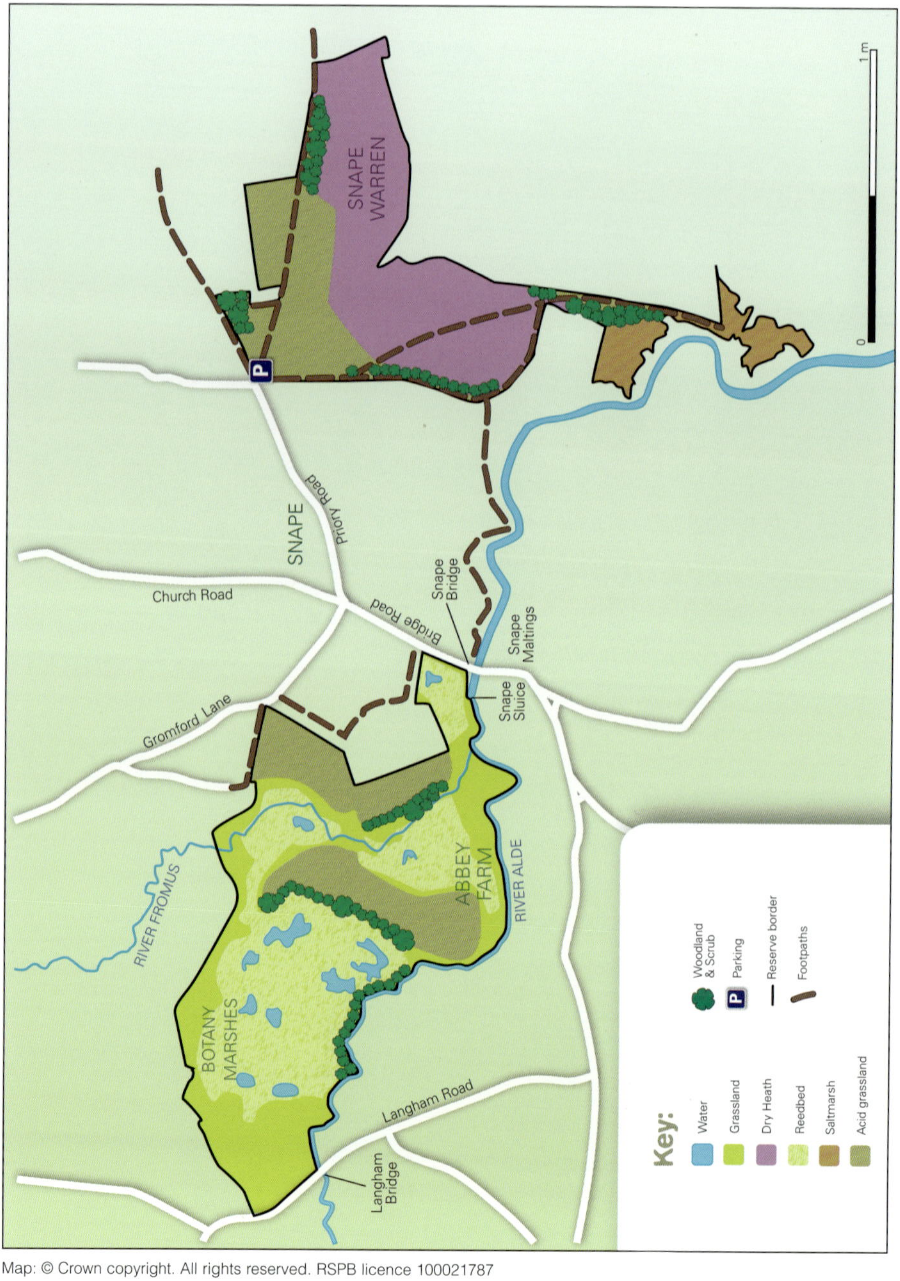

STEEPED IN HISTORY: Abbey Farm is part of the Alde Valley, an area with a rich and fascinating past. Its future is now assured as an important nature reserve. Inset, grey herons are often to be seen here.

Main photo: AARON HOWE, inset, JOHN BRIDGES (rspb-images.com)

Geography and history

The Snape Reserve is on the northern bank of the River Alde between Aldeburgh and Langham Bridge. The river and its estuary have, over the ages, witnessed generations of people and goods coming and going with the ebb and flow of the tide.

The reserve is split into separate areas – heathland and saltmarsh on Snape Warren and new wetlands upstream of Snape Bridge.

Snape Warren is an excellent example of a remaining fragment of the once-extensive Suffolk Sandlings heath, with patches of woodland on stony and sandy soils. It rises gently from reedbeds and tidal mudflats to higher ground with stunning views of the estuary towards Iken Cliffs and St Botolph's Church on the south bank. The reserve has quiet corners, places which feel remote, where stunted oaks grow close to the water or where a nightingale may sing from brambles at your feet.

Upstream from Snape Bridge, where the sluice marks the present limits of the tidal flow, is the RSPB-Environment Agency wetland creation project on Abbey Farm and Botany Marshes. Public access is limited at present while the habitats develop, but parts of the reserve are visible from public rights of way.

The marshes follow the alluvial valley of the Alde, and its tributary the Fromus, as it winds inland to Langham Bridge. The land rises imperceptibly above the sand, silt and occasional peat deposits of the valley bottom to the sandy, stony and well-drained ground of the original fields.

As the new habitats develop, RSPB Snape and other adjacent nature reserves will become an increasingly important wildlife corridor providing a safe haven, at a time of climate change, for a wide variety of rare and endangered wildlife.

The history of the Alde Valley is intimately bound up with the history of this east-facing coast of Britain. From the earliest times humans have sought out light, easily-managed soils, especially on south-facing slopes.

Archaeological finds in the area tell us that Bronze Age Britons, Romans and Anglo-Saxons came to the estuary and the river valleys beyond. The remains of Roman salt pans have been found on the banks of the Alde estuary.

At Snape Common, close to Snape Warren, local Anglo-Saxons put their pagan ship burial (resembling the better-known one at Sutton Hoo) among existing Bronze Age burial mounds. Downstream from Snape Warren at Barber's Point, on the banks of Ham Creek, an extensive, presumably Christian, Saxon cemetery has recently been excavated.

There is evidence of a Roman bath house and both Anglo-Saxon and medieval water mills in the vicinity of Langham Bridge, which appears to have been the upper tidal limit of the estuary and the lowest easily-fordable river crossing at that time. This was before the building of the river walls at Botany and Abbey farms to reclaim land from the estuary. A timber-framed medieval barn at Abbey Farm is the only remaining fragment of Snape Abbey, founded in 1155 by William Martell. It lasted until it was dissolved by Cardinal Wolsey to provide funds for his short-lived Cardinal College in Ipswich. It is likely that the abbey was involved in the building of the first wooden Snape Bridge, the forerunner of today's important crossing at the navigable head of the Alde.

A fascinating piece of modern history, linked to the Alde estuary and to the cultural life of the nation, is Snape Maltings. Snape was already a busy port when Newson Garrett of Aldeburgh built a maltings on the quayside for the processing and then export of locally grown barley. In addition a railway link to the main East Coast line was constructed in 1880 and, although closed in 1960, its remains are evident today and its course can be traced across both Botany and Abbey Farm marshes.

Much of the complex of distinguished Victorian buildings was unused when the composer Benjamin Britten realised that the main maltings building could be converted into a much-needed concert hall for the Aldeburgh Festival. Thus began the cultural, leisure, residential and retail complex of the present Snape Maltings.

INTERNATIONALLY ACCLAIMED: The famed Snape Maltings, with its impressive concert hall and retail complex, is a near-neighbour to the reserves and is viewed here from Snape Warren.

Photo: MALCOLM KEY

AT HOME IN THE SNOW: Grazing by hardy Exmoor ponies is an important reserve management feature at Snape Warren.

Habitats and management

Snape Warren

Since 2004 this 75 hectare (ha), once-neglected, heathland site has been transformed. RSPB staff and volunteers, including those from the RSPB Woodbridge Local Group, have worked together to create an attractive open habitat of heather, acid grassland and gorse with areas of woodland in which wildlife can flourish.

The heath has been opened up by clearing a smothering layer of scrub, felling dense areas of silver birch and spraying and cutting invasive bracken. Rabbits can now maintain the acid grassland, with occasional help from Exmoor and Dartmoor ponies and rare-breed Manx Loghtan sheep. The heather management has so far been by topping (mowing) in rotation, but controlled burning is an option for the future.

Abbey Farm and Botany Marshes

In 2007 the RSPB, with Environment Agency funding, purchased 100ha of dried-out grazing marsh at Abbey Farm, later adding Botany Marshes. This represents a symbolic step in the battle against climate change on the East Coast, whereby new reserves are being established in anticipation of habitat loss elsewhere.

New reedbeds are already emerging to attract the bitterns, bearded tits and marsh harriers which will inevitably be displaced as the sea encroaches on the reedbeds of existing reserves such as Minsmere and Dingle Marshes. On the rising ground, acid grassland is being managed for ground-nesting species such as stone-curlew, woodlark and skylark.

The marshes were ecologically depleted at the time of purchase. In the past, the low-lying parts were water meadows used as grazing marshes. The drainage ditches were then alive with plant and animal life and the annual cycle of grazing and hay-cutting encouraged a great variety of plant, and therefore animal, species in the meadows. All this was lost with the decline of traditional agriculture.

Already, on Abbey Farm, the RSPB has begun work raising water levels to give nature a helping hand. The original drains have been restored and sluices added, creating areas of open water and the reeds are spreading rapidly from the old ditch margins to create new reedbeds.

Each year the amount of wet reedbed is naturally increasing, up to an area of around 17ha, providing perfect conditions for breeding bitterns to colonise, as well as the full range of reedbed birds such as reed and sedge warblers, reed buntings and bearded tits.

At its margins, the reedbed grades into wet grassland with patches of open water. The attractive soft natural edges are maintained by Konik ponies and Highland cattle, which graze and trample the grass and reeds to create the tussocky, uneven surface which attracts ground-nesting birds such as redshank and lapwing.

Where the land rises, the former arable fields are reverting rapidly to acid grassland through a process of natural regeneration, combined with a regime of mowing and grazing by cattle, Exmoor ponies or rare-breed sheep such as Manx Loghtan or Wiltshire horn. Skylarks are already nesting here and management to attract stone-curlews will include creating strips and patches of rough and disturbed ground by rotovating each spring.

Looking out from the high ground on Abbey Farm onto the present grazing meadows of Botany Marshes, you can imagine a future landscape of reedbeds with stretches of open water between the low-lying fields. This will be a watery landscape, supplied by natural springs and by the River Fromus, whose tree-lined margin is visible in the distance.

Once the drainage ditches have been restored, ponds dug out and sluices installed, a new reedbed will be planted from specially-grown seedlings, and the renewal of this landscape and its wildlife can begin.

The work at Abbey Farm and Botany Marshes required a good deal of preparation and planning. There was initial survey work on the habitats, their geology and hydrology, and on populations of specific animals and plants. From this a 25-year plan emerged, setting out the vision and management objectives for these two sites.

Already, after only a few years of management at Abbey Farm, there are 51 species of breeding birds there, compared to 13 species at Botany Marshes. This indicates not only the wildlife potential of the new reserves, but also the success of the RSPB's management techniques.

Photo: MIKE PAGE

BESIDE THE ALDE: Snape Warren has extensive areas of heathland on light, dry soil.

PERFECT HABITAT: The heathland areas of Snape Warren, main photo, are home to species such as common blue butterfly, above, and grass snake, right.

Fauna

Snape Warren

These extensive areas of heathland on light, dry soil provide the perfect habitat for several of the UK's common reptiles. Adders and common lizards slither or scuttle away when disturbed on a sunny day. Grass snakes and slow worms are less easy to find and prefer the wooded areas where there is more undergrowth. Rabbits and small mammals contribute to the diet of foxes and badgers and muntjac, and the occasional fallow deer, may be encountered.

Heathland butterflies such as small heath, small copper, common and holly blue, grayling and the occasional white admiral are easy to spot on dry sunny days. Glow worms glow on summer evenings and the small pits of the antlion larvae, well known in the reserves on this coast, are also found here.

Abbey Farm and Botany Marshes

In the quiet backwaters of the River Alde, upstream from Snape Bridge and its tributary the Fromus, there is little to disturb some of our most secretive mammals and reptiles. Otters, water voles and several varieties of bat hunt and feed in or over these waters and their numbers are expected to increase as the reserve develops.

Many of the bats roost by day in the buildings at Snape Maltings, emerging at dusk to hunt insects over the water. Already, serotine, pipistrelle and barbastelle, one of the rarest bats in the UK, have been detected here. Their supersonic squeaks are identified by specialist bat detectors and the bats are easily visible against the evening sky.

There are few rabbits and few foxes, but there are well-established badger setts, with occasional sightings of the animals at dusk.

A considerable population of grass snakes and common lizards already exists at Abbey Farm, taking advantage of warm, south-facing banks, hedgerows and the river wall. A surprising number of first-year snakes are found around heaps of rotting vegetation, suggesting that this is the site of egg-laying and incubation.

The presence of so many snakes demands a good food supply and this is likely to be provided by young frogs and toads, as well as a large number of toad tadpoles, found in the River Fromus during the site surveys. Good numbers of Norfolk hawker dragonflies can be seen flying over the water in summer suggesting that the river is already supporting a wide range of other freshwater invertebrates. Butterflies also are on the increase as their food plants multiply, with species such as comma, common blue, meadow brown and ringlet seen in the fields and hedgerows.

There are already good populations of small freshwater fish and the rare brook lamprey occurs in the Fromus. Elvers have been imported from the River Severn to boost the eel population, a species traditionally found in East Anglian rivers. This creation of a healthy ecosystem should significantly increase the chances of attracting bitterns to the reserve, as their key food species will be present.

NEW COLONIST: Norfolk hawker dragonflies can be seen in good numbers during the summer months.

Flora

Snape Warren

The wide stretch of heath, with its groups of mature silver birch trees and well-shaped medium-sized oaks, is at its best in high summer. Patches of yellow gorse and bright purple bell heather can be found among the softer-coloured ling heather, which extends across the heath. In the areas of acid grassland, where bent grass and sheep's fescue dominate, the flowers of viper's bugloss and harebell give a touch of blue and extensive patches of flowering sheep's sorrel add splashes of bright red. A few other flowering plants such as heath bedstraw, biting stonecrop, the rare mossy stonecrop and common stork's bill can survive the desiccation which is common in summer on these well-drained, sandy soils.

HEATHLAND MIX: Heather and gorse are prominent features of the landscape at Snape Warren reserve.

In the patches of old woodland along the footpath to the river, small oaks dominate with hawthorn, blackthorn and woodland plants, such as honeysuckle and cow-wheat, between the bramble and bracken undergrowth. Close to the river the path crosses the saltmarsh, where tidal reedbeds are enlivened by patches of colour from flowering plants according to the season. The pink sea milkwort and white dittander of early summer are replaced later on by pink marsh mallow, purple sea aster and sea lavender with the green spikes of sea plantain alongside them.

Transformation of the Suffolk coast

Profile: Rob Macklin, A Man of Vision

Rob Macklin has been a warden, a site manager and an area manager for the RSPB and has always been a man with a vision. In his 25 years on the Suffolk coast he made a huge contribution to the development of the RSPB reserves, but has now moved on to new challenges in the West Country.

He came to Minsmere in 1986, after working for the RSPB in Wales, Orkney and on the south coast of England. In those early days there were no job descriptions and Rob flourished, turning his hand to anything and everything, which was a great asset when clearing up after the 1987 'Great Storm'.

As site manager of RSPB North Warren and Aldringham Walks Reserve from 1990, the vision was the re-wetting of the dried-out reedbeds to recreate the wet reedbed and mere and bring back the bitterns, marsh harriers and bearded tits. After the earth-moving machinery had left and the reeds had re-established themselves, the reward for Rob, *pictured,* was the first sound of booming bitterns for many years.

Perhaps Rob's greatest contribution has been made since 2003, when he became the RSPB's area manager for the Suffolk coast. The vision now was to increase the amount of land under RSPB supervision, either by land purchase or by leasing or management agreements.

Snape Marshes and Hollesley Marshes were established as new reserves. Abbey Farm and Botany Marshes at Snape were purchased by the Environment Agency to compensate for anticipated future losses of coastal reedbeds to the sea, with the RSPB responsible for the management of these sites to create thriving new freshwater reedbeds.

More recently, Rob was closely involved with a joint project with the Forestry Commission and Suffolk Wildlife Trust to return Dunwich Forest to its pre-plantation landscape. The RSPB is re-establishing heathland in areas that have been clear-felled, while Suffolk Wildlife Trust returns other areas to wood pasture.

Rob accepts that the time of big land acquisitions is over for the RSPB and that collaboration with farmers and land owners must be the way forward.

This is a core element of RSPB Futurescapes, which aims to halt the decline in numbers of farmland birds and to increase biodiversity by encouraging wildlife-friendly practices as part of normal farming activity.

Intensive agriculture, increases in population, changing climate patterns, water shortages and rising sea levels are all putting pressure on wildlife in East Anglia.

Rob's vision for the Suffolk coast was of a network of environmentally rich corridors such as hedgerows, uncultivated field margins and woods and heaths, linking our reserves and wildlife-rich farms. Through these routes our birds, mammals, and insects can move, migrate and spread around the countryside extending their ranges from the isolated refuges of the nature reserves.

The two species that best sum up Rob's legacy on the Suffolk coast are the bittern and the stone-curlew. Through his long-term planning and practical work, creating wetlands for the bittern and dry grassland and heathland for the stone-curlew, both species are now well-established on the Suffolk coast.

The bonus is that other species have followed. Marsh harriers, hobbies, bearded tits, otters and little egrets are increasingly common in the reedbeds and, on the heaths, nightjars, woodlarks and the silver-studded blue butterflies flourish. These changes all celebrate the renewal, under Rob's management, of the richness of the Suffolk coast.

Abbey Farm and Botany Marshes

The regenerating reedbeds and the network of ditches through the wet meadows at Abbey Farm already contain an interesting variety of water plants suchas flowering rush, water plantain, yellow iris, figwort and valerian. In some areas of open water yellow water-lilies are established. Many of these plants will extend their range as the improvements to the reedbeds and wet grassland further upstream at Botany Marshes are completed.

SPECIAL SPECIES: The scarce flowering rush thrives in the damper areas at Abbey Farm.

The tributary river, the Fromus, with its clear water, has good patches of reeds with arrowhead, branched bur-reed and watercress along its banks. The water meadows have, until recently, been dominated by coarse grasses with docks and thistles. With the management regime of cutting and grazing the colourful hay meadows have returned, with yellow rattle, ragged robin and southern marsh orchid flowering among the meadow grasses such as Yorkshire fog and rye grass.

On the drier acid grassland, the fescue grasses and bent grasses are appearing among the drought-tolerant flowering plants such as bugloss and cudweed. Patches of creeping thistle provide an excellent nectar source for butterflies and other insects.

There is little natural woodland on either Abbey Farm or Botany Marshes, apart from planted hedges. A dense area of recently planted hedgerow with spindle, rowan and other berry-bearing trees and shrubs is being managed to attract bullfinches and turtle doves.

Wildlife Season by Season

WINTER: DECEMBER, JANUARY, FEBRUARY

Snape Warren

Visitors during the winter months will hear few birds as they walk through the heaths and woods, apart from an occasional Dartford warbler calling from the tops of the gorse. A short-eared owl may quarter over the heather and a passing hen harrier may linger for a day or two.

As you approach the reedbed, bearded tits or reed buntings may be calling and a barn owl or marsh harrier may be hunting over the reeds. By the river, the silence may be punctuated by the haunting sounds of redshanks, curlews and oystercatchers.

The rich food sources here attract large numbers of winter migrants, mainly waders and ducks, which join the feral Canada and greylag geese on this sheltered, south-facing shoreline. On the water at high tide, rafts of wigeons and groups of shelducks, with smaller numbers of pintails and teals, can be seen.

As the tide falls, lapwings may rise in quivering flocks from feeding on the mud. Smaller parties of dunlins may dart and bank, flashing their white underparts before settling at the water's edge.

The fortunate birdwatcher may detect a glowing line of black-and-white avocets across the water on an exposed mud bank, or hear their fluting calls as they fly in line up or downstream. Another unforgettable experience is the sight of a flock of black-tailed godwits in flight, their wing-bars and tail-bars catching the light.

A SOUND OF SPRING: Male Dartford warblers issue their scratchy song at Snape Warren.

Abbey Farm and Botany Marshes

Curlews and black-tailed godwits have discovered the new wetland habitat provided at Abbey Farm and Botany Marshes with between 200 and 300 of each species roosting there at different times during the winter, usually at high tide.

Golden plovers and lapwings are also using the reserve as a winter haven and these are being joined by increasing numbers of wigeons, teals and pintails.

Small mammals are prey for the resident barn owl that is often seen quartering the ground on a winter afternoon and also for the kestrels that take advantage of the short hours of daylight to hover over the grassland.

Other recent winter highlights are sightings of common snipe, jack snipe, water rails, marsh harriers and bearded tits – a foretaste, we hope, of future developments.

Spring: March, April, May

Snape Warren

The sounds of spring begin early in the sheltered pockets of woodland around the heath. From deep in the undergrowth the explosive song of a Cetti's warbler emerges and, as the chiffchaffs begin their rhythmic call, the yaffle of a green woodpecker fills the air. On the heath, a Dartford warbler may call from a gorse-top perch, linnets sing to establish their territories and the fluting notes of a woodlark can be compared with the more familiar song of a soaring skylark over the grassland.

From the saltmarsh, looking out over the estuary, you may glimpse passage migrants, such as whimbrels, bar-tailed godwits, greenshanks and spotted redshanks. Flocks of avocets, curlews and black-tailed godwits remain until early May.

As the migrant songbirds return in April and

Main photo: JOHN BRIDGES (rspb-images.com), inset, ANDY HAY (rspb-images.com)

SUMMER VISITORS: Common whitethroat, main photo, and the not-so-common turtle dove, inset, return to the area to breed and their songs are among the delights of visits to the Snape area.

May, nightingales sing to establish their territories where the brambles are thickest. The flowing songs of blackcaps and garden warblers are heard from the trees and common whitethroats call and fly from their perches in the scrub.

A total of 37 species breed on the reserve, including increasing numbers of turtle doves, a good population of skylarks, a fluctuating smaller population of woodlarks and a few pairs of nightjars. Yellowhammers, linnets and reed buntings have thriving breeding populations.

Abbey Farm and Botany Marshes

Springtime reveals the fantastic potential of these marshes. At present they are tranquil, undisturbed places with new habitats progressively emerging and wildlife moving in.

Temporary spring visitors on their way north are pausing to feed for a few days. On the flooded fields at Abbey Farm, wood, green and common sandpipers may be seen.

Marsh harriers bred here for the first time in 2011 and can regularly be seen hunting over the marshes. Bearded tits often linger into spring and bitterns are occasionally seen. The reserve managers are expecting both these species to stay and breed.

Several pairs of lapwings and redshanks have already nested. Some of the wintering ducks, such as teals and gadwalls, are staying on to breed and the first mallard chicks are on display. However, the real success story is in the reedbed and other wet areas where outstanding numbers of reed buntings and Cetti's, reed and sedge warblers are now established breeders. It may be no coincidence that this is now a stronghold for cuckoos locally, despite big regional declines.

There has been a surge in numbers of breeding resident species such as dunnock, robin and wren and also of migrant songbirds such as whitethroat, blackcap and chiffchaff. Skylarks and woodlarks are already nesting in the drier areas at Abbey Farm and should do so in the regenerating grassland at Botany Marshes.

Photo: JOHN BRIDGES (rspb-images.com)

THRILLING SIGHT: Kingfishers are occasionally encountered around the area's wetlands.

SUMMER: JUNE, JULY, AUGUST

Snape Warren

By mid-summer, the reserve is a more tranquil place. Families of linnets may be calling and flitting through the gorse on the heaths and the heather is in full bloom. This is the best time of year to catch sight of adders and lizards on bare patches of sandy soil among the heather. On warm, still evenings in June and July look out for the glow worms and listen for the churring calls of nightjars as the birds flutter along the woodland edges.

On the estuary, broods of shelduck chicks gather on the water and avocets, redshanks and black-tailed godwits assemble to feed as their breeding is completed and the autumn migration begins. Young marsh harriers may be on the wing and little egrets are feeding in the marshes as the sea aster and sea lavender begin to flower.

Abbey Farm and Botany Marshes

As the summer progresses in the reedbeds, the number of birds and the noise of their chatter will increase as the young fledge. Reed bunting and sedge and reed warbler young communicate noisily, but unseen, deep in the wet vegetation. Herons feed in the reedbed edges and draw our attention as they fly away into the distance.

From their nesting sites at the Maltings, house martins are hunting over the reserve for insects and groups of young swifts perform aerobatics before suddenly departing at the beginning of August. Swallows from the barn at Abbey Farm will join them and an occasional hobby may swoop after dragonflies. This is a good time to see the resident barn owl and marsh harriers with their young, hunting over the marshes.

AUTUMN: SEPTEMBER, OCTOBER, NOVEMBER

Snape Warren

As the autumn draws in, the heath and the woods remain quiet but the estuary demonstrates its importance for waders and wildfowl as a diverse range of passage migrants use it as a staging post on their way south to their winter feeding grounds. Flocks of knots and golden plovers call in, stay for a while and then move on, while dunlins, avocets, black-tailed godwits, lapwings and curlews may stay for longer and many will be around throughout the winter.

At dusk look out for the flocks of starlings which have become a regular feature over the estuary. The birds gather from miles away before settling to roost in the reedbeds as darkness falls.

Abbey Farm and Botany Marshes

The autumn brings a wider range of visitors to the marshes. Little egrets, mute swans and common snipe are frequently around in the pools or the wet grassland. The numbers of wildfowl and waders build up, with wigeons, teals, curlews, black-tailed godwits and lapwings regularly gathering at high tide. Kingfishers are quite frequently seen around Snape Bridge and further upstream.

RESERVE INFORMATION

Opening times

Access to Snape Warren is at all times via public footpaths. Most of Snape Warren is also Open Access. Access to Abbey Farm and Botany Marshes is via occasional guided walks only at present. Please check the website for details of events and future access arrangements.

How to get there

From the A12 on the A1094 towards Aldeburgh, then turn right onto B1069. Turn left at The Crown pub into Priory Lane. After about half a mile, at sharp left bend, fork right and a small car park is on right after 10 metres. Alternatively, walk east along north bank of the River Alde from Snape Maltings. You can view the edge of Abbey Farm from Snape Bridge.

Facilities

- Small car park with information board.
- Parking, shops, pub, cafés and toilets at Snape Maltings.
- Pubs and a shop/post office in Snape village.

Further information

Contact: RSPB Havergate and Snape office, tel: 01394 450732; email: snape@rspb.org.uk or see www.rspb.org.uk/snape

Havergate

Island of the avocet

AT THE JETTY: Visitors by boat can see avocets, inset, as soon as they arrive.

Geography and history

Havergate Island, Suffolk's only island, lies in a stretch of the Alde/Ore estuary that was once open sea. More than 1,000 years' accumulation of sand and shingle has formed the spit of land we now call Orford Ness and which encloses Havergate in the long, narrow estuary running from Aldeburgh to Shingle Street.

Havergate today is a little under two miles long and covers 108 hectares. It consists of two original islands joined by a shingle bank and is covered mainly by shallow lagoons containing small islands and mudflats for breeding birds and wintering wildfowl and waders.

Although below sea level and at risk from flooding by the increasingly high tides, it is protected by river walls first begun by local people over 500 years ago. Inside these, farmers were able to drain and improve the land.

There is evidence from the ridge-and-furrow patterns still visible in some of the lagoons that crops such as vegetables and cereals were grown, but cattle grazing became the prime use. The cattle were brought over by a barge, half of which is still visible near Orford Quay, to the north of the island.

The remains of a cottage and garden, where the farmers and their families lived, could be seen until recently. We know from records and from local memories that the Brinkley family, and then a Mr Welham and his housekeeper, lived in a cottage on the island from 1865 to the late 1920s when they were employees of the then owner, a Mr Fiske. Faded photographs from before the Second World War show members of the Fiske family outside the cottage.

Throughout the 1930s cattle were still brought to the island for summer grazing and then, in 1933, a gravel company began to exploit Havergate as a source of shingle, removing part of the shingle ridge joining the two halves of the island.

Smugglers took advantage of the island's isolation. Local folklore tells of the Havergate shepherd, in league with the smugglers, who signalled with lights in the cottage window that the coast was clear for them to land their contraband on the deserted Ness and ferry the illicit goods onto the island. After such a landing the shepherd would drive his sheep up and down on the foreshore to hide the tell-tale signs of activity.

At the Jolly Sailor Inn, near Orford Quay, you can see a poster telling the story of the

Suffolk maidservant Margaret Catchpole. She fell in love with one of the smugglers and, for his sake, stole a horse and rode it from Ipswich to London. In March 1800 a £20.00 reward was offered for her capture. By 1801, the unfortunate young woman was caught, tried and transported to Australia.

The Second World War played a decisive role in the future of Havergate. Situated near the most easterly point of England, the area's isolation was combined with vulnerability to attack and invasion. The result for Havergate was benign neglect. The land flooded with sea water, access for farm animals and people was denied, and a safe haven for breeding and wintering birds was created.

Avocets returned to breed on the island in 1947 after an absence from the UK of more than 100 years. The species had previously suffered persecution but the future for the avocet, and for all Havergate's wildlife, was assured by the RSPB's purchase of the island in 1948 – and the avocet became the society's emblem.

The purchase also began the association of the Partridge family with Havergate and its development as an RSPB reserve. Under the wardenships of Reg, his son John and their successors, Havergate has acquired an international reputation – it is a Site of Special Scientific Interest, a National Nature Reserve and a Ramsar site. The island is within the Suffolk Coast and Heaths Area of Outstanding Natural Beauty and on the Suffolk Heritage Coast.

Between 25 and 30 bird species breed here and in any one year about 150 species are recorded. Rats, foxes and, above all, the weather have created problems on the island. Hurricane force winds in 1953, 1983, 1987 and 2007 caused havoc, wrecking sea defences along the coast, submerging Havergate and breaching the river walls.

A reminder of the 1953 storm is the marker post near the accommodation huts on the island showing the high-water mark of the floods. This is the highest point on the island, so the upperparts of the huts and the river wall were all that could be seen above the water.

At the height of this storm, the warden Reg Partridge summoned his reserves of strength

ISLAND FROM ABOVE: An aerial view of Havergate Island, looking north, with the spit of Orford Ness to the right and Butley River running off to the left near the southern end of the island.

Photo: MIKE PAGE

and experience to rescue in his small boat two security policemen from the Atomic Weapons Research Establishment who were stranded on Orford Ness. He won the British Empire medal for his courage.

The reserve has survived challenges such as these over the years thanks to heroic efforts by the Partridges and local volunteers, including those from the RSPB Woodbridge Local Group. The river walls have been made wider and higher to cope with rising sea levels and hides have been refurbished and rebuilt.

UNIQUE ATMOSPHERE: Havergate Island has a distinctive character – it is Suffolk's only island.

Habitats and management

Punctuated by these emergencies, the management and maintenance of the reserve as a major wetland area has continued. A joint project between RSPB Havergate Island and Orford Ness National Trust is being funded by EU LIFE+, a European funding programme, to benefit protected species and habitats.

There are major changes to some of the lagoons to improve the view from the hides. The topography of the lagoons has been changed to give a wider range of water depths and a variety of sloping shorelines to the islands. The tidal sluices, which control the circulation of seawater flowing through the lagoons from north to south, have been renovated and enlarged to achieve better salinity control.

Water salinity is monitored regularly to keep it close to the 3.5% salt and mineral content of the estuary and sea water, thus providing appropriate conditions for the invertebrates such as Corophium shrimps, Chironomid midge larvae and ragworms, on which the birds feed.

There are five hides overlooking the original fields of Havergate which have been transformed into six artificial lagoons with the deeper water at the edges marking the positions of the traditional 'borrow' dykes around each field. The clay dug from these ditches is 'borrowed' to make the river walls.

There are some 200 artificial shingle and mud islands in the lagoons. They provide nesting and roosting sites for waders, ducks and terns. The islands are covered in vegetation such as couch grass, but erode gradually due to wave action and must be regularly rebuilt.

Water levels are monitored to avoid flooding or drying out and varied season by season. The levels are raised slightly in winter, thus killing the vegetation on the islands' edges to create muddy or stony shores and are kept high in spring to ensure the birds make their nests high on the islands. Once nest sites are established, the levels are dropped to reduce flooding risks. In late spring the levels are dropped again to provide optimum feeding conditions for young and migrating birds.

Throughout autumn and winter, management work concentrates on creating ideal conditions for nesting and feeding on the islands. Islands accessible by tractor are mown in the autumn to provide a short growth for winter grazing of ducks and geese and create the rough, short vegetation preferred as nesting sites by lapwings and redshanks the following spring.

Some islands are left untouched to provide the cover favoured by ducks such as mallards, shovelers and tufted ducks. Vegetation covering low-lying islands can be killed by raising the water levels. This is done because many wading birds, such as avocets, oystercatchers and ringed plovers, together with terns, prefer clear ground for their nests.

Although the lagoons and islands are the major habitats of the reserve, there is saltmarsh around the lagoons and around the island in a narrow band outside the river walls. The remains of the shingle bank which still links the southern, smaller island of Dovey's to the main island is an important site for rare spiders and plants.

Two small areas of gorse provide an important breeding habitat for linnets and, in winter, provide shelter for the island's hare population and migrant species such as blackbird, robin, reed bunting and goldcrest.

With the threat of rising sea levels affecting this estuary reserve, the crumbling of the defences at the northern end of the island led to Havergate's contribution to 'managed realignment'. The river wall was deliberately breached in 2000, flooding an area of grassland in Cuckolds Marsh so that saltmarsh could be restored. This project required complex planning – checking on existing water levels and drainage and listing existing flora and fauna – and follow-up survey work on accretion rates, erosion and changes in invertebrate populations.

Visitors will see that nature is taking its course. The tide sweeps in and out depositing mud, smoothing its surface, making new channels and flow patterns and creating new feeding areas for the probing beaks of waders. A biological succession is beginning to follow, with colonising plants on the highest banks, trapping the mud and raising the land levels to create new saltmarsh – a habitat for breeding waders such as redshank and a natural defence against storm and flood.

Photos: IAN BARTHORPE

DIGGERS AT WORK: Major habitat improvements were made over the winter of 2011/12.

Havergate

Main photo: MATTHEW GUILLETT (National Trust), inset, EAST ANGLIAN DAILY TIMES

HARE IN THE AIR: Brown hares often enthral visitors to the island and in early spring their antics are a particular spectacle.

Fauna

Brown hares were originally introduced to the island as a source of food and now they number about 50. They are attractive to visitors and, as plant-eaters, harmless to birds. Rats and foxes, however, are not welcome as they prey on the eggs and young of nesting birds. Water and field voles, common and water shrews have all been recorded and are the main diet of the short-eared owls that hunt the island's grasslands.

Photo: DAVID FAIRHURST

The most common of the 17 recorded species of butterfly is the Essex skipper. Other species regularly seen include small skipper, meadow brown, common blue, wall brown, red admiral, peacock and small tortoiseshell. In some years painted lady and clouded yellow butterflies arrive from Europe and settle on the island.

Many other insects, including common darter and migrant hawker dragonflies, can be seen on the island in summer, but the lack of freshwater pools prevents successful breeding.

The very localised ground lackey is among the moths on the reserve and on sunny days in late summer visitors may hear the hissing 'song' of the Röesel's bush cricket.

PURPLE HAZE: Sea lavender sets the island ablaze with colour, main photo. English stonecrop, left, and sea campion, right, add to Havergate's botanic interest. Below, a bumblebee makes itself busy on a sprig of sea lavender.

Flora

The 134 species of plant on the island are typical of an estuarine habitat with clay soil, shingle and high-level saltmarsh.

The most interesting are on the shingle bank, south of the accommodation huts, and on the high-level saltmarsh. In midsummer these areas abound in saltmarsh grass, scurvy grass, sea purslane, marsh samphire, thrift, sea lavender and sea spurrey. On the shingle bank are herb robert, (yellow) biting stonecrop, English stonecrop, yellow vetch, sea campion, and the very localised sea pea. Sea wormwood can be found at the foot of the river banks. Near Dovey's lagoon there are small patches of native cord grass and patches of reed line the borrow dykes.

On the artificial mud and shingle islands in the lagoons the dominant plant is sea purslane interspersed with couch grass and patches of the invasive, woody and unattractive grass-leaved orache. The latter also grows in unwelcome profusion on the river walls.

The Duke of Argyll's tea plant that is found on the island is perhaps a legacy from the old cottage garden and there is tamarisk which must also have been introduced.

Reserve reflections: special memories of Havergate

Three Partridges

ISLAND MAN: Reg Partridge, Havergate's first full-time warden for the reserve.

"When the avocets were first recorded at Havergate, watchers set up a continuous guard on them. They camped in tents near today's living quarters. Two local men, a Mr Groves and a Mr Hornsby, were connected with the RSPB and formed a committee to oversee operations.

They employed Theo Harvey to ferry watchers to and from the island but after Theo died Mr Hornsby asked Reg Partridge to take over the job. A short time later Reg was taken on by the RSPB as full-time warden.

There were no voluntary wardens staying on the island in those early years so Reg and I would spend time there, particularly during the breeding season. My role was to greet visitors and look after them until Reg had moored the boat and come ashore.

The accommodation then was two very basic huts, one for living and cooking in, the other for sleeping. Cooking was done on two paraffin stoves and there were very few other comforts. Our son John would also stay during the summer holidays and the headmaster of the local school would let him join us at times during term time as he classed it as education. John spent many hours on the island with Reg, standing him in good stead when he took over the wardenship.

Things were a little 'ad-hoc' in those days. I remember during the Suez Crisis fuel was in short supply. When Reg got low on his ration he rigged up a sail on his boat and sailed to the reserve.

In the great floods of 1953 Reg and a band of local helpers spent days and days repairing sea wall breaches and I remember this was done by filling hundreds of sandbags by hand and carrying them into place. However, the job was completed in time so that the avocets could safely nest during the summer. My involvement with Havergate with Reg, then John, has spanned 55 years and has been very enjoyable."

Ettie Partridge

Wildlife season by season

WINTER: DECEMBER, JANUARY, FEBRUARY

The avocet may be the most famous of Havergate's birds with up to 1,000 now wintering, making the estuary an internationally important winter roosting site, but it is by no means the most numerous of the island's 150 species.

Every visitor has their favourite season on the island but most will agree that, for sheer numbers of birds, a winter visit never ceases to amaze and inspire. Between October and March large flocks of ducks and waders are feeding in the lagoons, rising and wheeling round as huge clouds from time to time.

A flock of avocets on Main or Dovey's lagoon disturbed by a predator, such as a buzzard, peregrine falcon or merlin, can fill the air with a fluttering mass of black and white which settles again within minutes as a thin, distant, white line. A cloud of dunlin flashing alternately light and dark moves low across the water and instantly vanishes.

During these months there are seldom fewer than 400 or 500 wigeons present. Often, in the coldest part of the winter, the total is well over 2,000. Wigeon is usually the most numerous duck species, with teal a good second, but visitors may also

ON THE ALERT: Short-eared owls are often seen hunting over Havergate Island's rough grassland.

expect to see up to 150 each of mallard, pintail and shoveler, while there are usually about 100 shelducks on the island throughout the year.

Wherever there is deeper water, groups of diving ducks feed – tufted ducks, pochards and goldeneyes, with the occasional smew or scaup disappearing under the water with frustrating frequency.

Feeding and roosting alongside the avocets there are between 10 and 15 other species of wader. Grey plovers are usually present in some numbers, together with knots, dunlins, common snipe, lapwings and redshanks.

The resident barn owls are often seen in winter, even hunting in daylight. Short-eared owls are frequent visitors and at least one hen harrier is usually around. A hovering kestrel is a common sight and, on the sluice gates, a perched kingfisher can often be seen.

SPRING: MARCH, APRIL, MAY

Spring may start as early as February with the first departures of the ducks. As the days lengthen, signs of the breeding season intensify with skylarks claiming their territory with song and redshank gliding on vibrating wings in courtship flight.

The true excitements of spring are seen in April as breeding birds migrate north from their winter feeding grounds further south in Europe, Africa or elsewhere. Fewer avocets are seen here as most return to breeding grounds in mainland Europe. Elegant black-tailed and bar-tailed godwits, with the beginnings of their dramatic chestnut breeding plumage, may stay for a few days en route for breeding grounds in northern Europe and inside the Arctic Circle.

Common, little and Sandwich terns return before the end of the month and may be seen on the other side of the river wall, following the shallows of the river, hovering, diving and occasionally rising from the water with fish in their beaks. Later, common terns and occasionally Sandwich terns, may establish nests in the shingle on Havergate or at nearby sites such as Orford Ness.

Many breeding birds defend their nesting territories with elaborate rituals. The tern displays are highly aggressive. The aim is to drive away rivals and, at the same time, to establish pair bonds with their mates. Male shelducks engage in aggressive head-bobbing towards rival males whereas oystercatchers defend their territories with shrill, far-carrying, piping calls and display with their bright red beaks open and held downward.

A frequent visitor in all seasons is the marsh harrier. At this time of year they may be nesting in nearby secluded areas, perhaps on Orford Ness or the upper reaches of the Butley River, and males and females will visit to hunt for prey for themselves and for their nestlings.

Wheatears and whinchats are regular passage migrants on Havergate, taking advantage of the short grass on the paths as they pass through on their way to northern upland areas of the UK and beyond.

A few pairs of avocets may attempt to breed but predation by herring and lesser black-backed gulls has increased to such an extent that most of the avocets have moved elsewhere to breed. There are now 500 herring gulls and 1,000 lesser black-backed gulls on Havergate – significant numbers for both species whose numbers are diminishing elsewhere.

Some late passage migrant species, such as whimbrel, greenshank, grey plover and turnstone, may still be encountered. By the end of May the saltmarsh and shingle are covered in pink clumps of flowering thrift. The last stragglers of over-wintering ducks have departed, though a few mallards and shovelers may stay to breed.

The northward passage of swallows, swifts, sand martins and house martins builds to a peak during May and groups of them may be seen hawking for insects over the lagoons. Two species which nest in nearby pine plantations, little egrets and grey herons, hunt for eels and small fish in the ditches at the edges of the lagoons.

SUMMER: JUNE, JULY, AUGUST

By June the main interest centres on breeding birds. The redshanks, ringed plovers, avocets and oystercatchers that breed on Havergate are feeding in the lagoons or resting on the islands. The breeding success of these ground-nesting birds is very dependent on the weather and the number of predators. Gulls, the occasional fox or continuous rain, can cause a great deal of trouble.

There are few other waders apart from dunlins. To compensate, the smaller birds which nest on the island – meadow pipits, skylarks, linnets and reed buntings – are much in evidence. The island provides perfect conditions for the barn owls which nest in the tractor shed and

ISLAND VISITORS: Sandwich terns, below, are now irregular breeders but common terns, inset, nest every year in a thriving colony.

Main photo: JON EVANS insets, GRAHAM THOMPSON

STAR ATTRACTION: Spoonbill, main photo, is a species for which Havergate Island is justifiably famous and it is one of the most reliable sites in the UK for this exotic visitor. Inset, far left, common gull defies its name but is a frequent breeder. Inset, left, herring gull still breeds in significant numbers on the island.

feed their young on the plentiful supply of small mammals in the rough grassland.

The raucous noise of the gull colonies on the shingle bank, in the saltmarsh and at Dovey's lagoon greets visitors to the island during the summer months. Good numbers of young have been reared by both lesser black-backed and herring gulls in recent years. There are a few pairs of great black-backed and common gulls. Indeed, Havergate is the most southerly breeding point in the UK for the latter species.

Look out in the saltmarshes for colourful clusters of ground lackey moth caterpillars, surrounded by their silk webs, as they feed on sea lavender and sea wormwood leaves. You may hear, but not see, the monotonous sound of the Röesel's bush cricket in the rough grass inside the river wall.

The picture changes again by July when many of the breeding birds have chicks which are almost fully grown. This increase in the number of birds makes July one of the most interesting months on the island and it also sees the start of the southward wader migration. Dunlin and ringed plover numbers increase, followed by turnstones, common sandpipers and knots. By the end of the month, green sandpipers and greenshanks may also be seen.

In recent years some more exotic visitors have arrived in early summer, when a group of around 20 spoonbills may be seen roosting or feeding around the lagoons. When they move around or fly, their impressive size and remarkable bills never fail to excite the onlookers. There is always the hope that, like the little egrets, they may one day nest around here.

By August, the breeding season is virtually over but the breeding birds are still very much on view against a backdrop of the rich, purple colour of sea lavender. Avocet numbers rise in August with an influx of adults and fledged young from other breeding grounds in the UK and Europe. They rest in groups along with redshanks, oystercatchers and young shelducks, whose parents have moved away to moult.

The early stages of return passage continue with the arrival in the second half of the month of other migrants on their way south. Bar-tailed and black-tailed godwits, curlews, whimbrels, turnstones, knots, greenshanks, common sandpipers and golden plovers are often present, with one or two curlew sandpipers and the occasional little stint among the dunlins.

The arrival of grey plovers and the first wigeons ends the month and signifies the end of summer.

AUTUMN: SEPTEMBER, OCTOBER, NOVEMBER

The yearly cycle is completed in September and October when the green stems of samphire develop their red autumnal colours, summer birds such as the terns depart and hirundines and other migrants pass through.

This is an exciting time on the reserve with constant surprises as passage migrants arrive, stay for a few days, and then move on. The arrival of a spotted redshank, a green or curlew sandpiper, a little stint, a sanderling or a group of ruffs is always a thrill.

Small flocks of goldfinches may arrive to feed on seeds of sea aster and thistle. The white rump of a wheatear along the river wall or the conspicuous colour of a yellow wagtail reveals the arrival of the first passerine migrants, which also include chiffchaffs, willow warblers and blackcaps.

Ducks increase in number, beginning with mallards and wigeons followed by pintails, shovelers and teals. They feed in the lagoons, occasionally flying up in huge flocks when disturbed by a passing peregrine falcon or merlin.

A sure sign of the season changing is the arrival of a kingfisher or the first wintering robins. Havergate's lagoons and islands are the perfect winter habitats for this rich variety of birds.

Photos: ANDY HAY (rspb-images.com)

WINTER INVASION: Flocks of wildfowl, including teal, left, and wigeon, above, arrive from northern and eastern Europe as the weather closes in.

Havergate Adventure

Since the 'Great Storm' in 1987, the RSPB Woodbridge Local Group have been organising the 'Havergate Adventure', bringing members of the public to the island on several days over the third weekend in August.

Originally, the aim was to raise funds to repair the devastating damage to the river wall, buildings, bridges and paths caused by winds and flooding. Now, as well as fund raising, we would like as many people as possible to experience the beauty of the avocets and the other rich birdlife of the island. A boat trip from Orford Quay to the island is followed by a two-hour guided tour, to view the birds from a series of hides. Families and children are welcome and there are home made refreshments and binoculars available for those who need them.

Information from www.rspb.org.uk/groups/woodbridge
Booking usually starts on August 1st

Reserve reflections: special memories of Havergate

Maintenance – a thumbnail sketch

“Enthusiasm for birds expresses itself in many ways; for those of us lucky enough to live near the enchanting Suffolk coast, where Minsmere and Havergate beckon, assisting wardens to manage these reserves is one rewarding option.

A hide repair work party was organised one February to replace unstable seating with benches.

The view from the hide we were working on was spellbinding – but work had to continue. Concentration was hard here with so much to see and then it happened! The darting flight of one of the island's latest arrivals distracted me and the hammer I was aiming at a monster nail missed and whacked my thumb instead! It was very painful, and black for many months, but the reward of seeing those newly arrived ringed plovers was worth it.”

Malcolm Key, volunteer worker

BIG HIT: The new arrival of ringed plovers was worth a bruised thumb for volunteer Malcolm Key.

PROFUSION OF WADERS: Havergate Island is renowned for its avocets and other wading birds including black-tailed godwit, above right, and common snipe, right.

Reserve reflections: special memories of Havergate

Eyes like a hawk

"One of my most treasured memories from the early days was being there at the time when Reg Partridge was warden.

At that time the summer warden always had Tuesdays off and that was when Reg might take the 'voluntary' for a spot of birdwatching. So my birdwatching was enhanced by a warden who had probably the best long sight in the business – Reg had eyes like a hawk. Why he bothered with binoculars I shall never know.

On one of these forays – it must have been in June – a spotted redshank in splendid summer plumage came over the bank and into the lagoon followed by a paler bird. I could identify the darker bird but the paler one was a puzzle so I asked Reg. 'That's one of nature's little tricks, they're both duskies, one's in summer plumage and the other's in winter garb' – Reg always used dialect words for birds."

Keith Bennett, *volunteer summer warden 1986 – 89*

Photo: IAN BARTHORPE

HOMEWARD BOUND: October Storm heads back to Orford Quay after another visit to Havergate Island.

RESERVE INFORMATION

Open dates

Boats to Havergate depart Orford Quay at 10 am on the first Saturday of every month, returning at about 3.30 pm. There are several special event weekends per year, with up to four trips per day. For details please check the website (see below). Please note that these arrangements are subject to change.

How to get there

The village of Orford is located 17km(11miles) North East of Woodbridge; the village is sign-posted off the A12. Follow the A1152 and then the B1084 to Orford. There is a large car park adjacent to the quay.

Cost

RSPB members £12
Non members £15
There is no child discount.
(Prices as at June 2012)

How to book

Access is by RSPB boat only. There are limited places on the boat so prior booking is essential. Bookings are taken through the visitor centre at RSPB Minsmere, tel: 01728 648281, open from 9am -5pm (1 February-31 October) and from 9am-4pm (1 November-31 January).

Facilities

- Five birdwatching hides.
- Viewing platform.
- Visitor reception centre.
- Picnic area.
- Public toilets.
- Visitor trail approx 2 km.
- Volunteer guides are often available to help you.

Further information

Contact: The Warden, email: havergate.island@rspb.org.uk or see www.rspb.org.uk/havergate

Boyton & Hollesley Marshes

Wetlands recovered

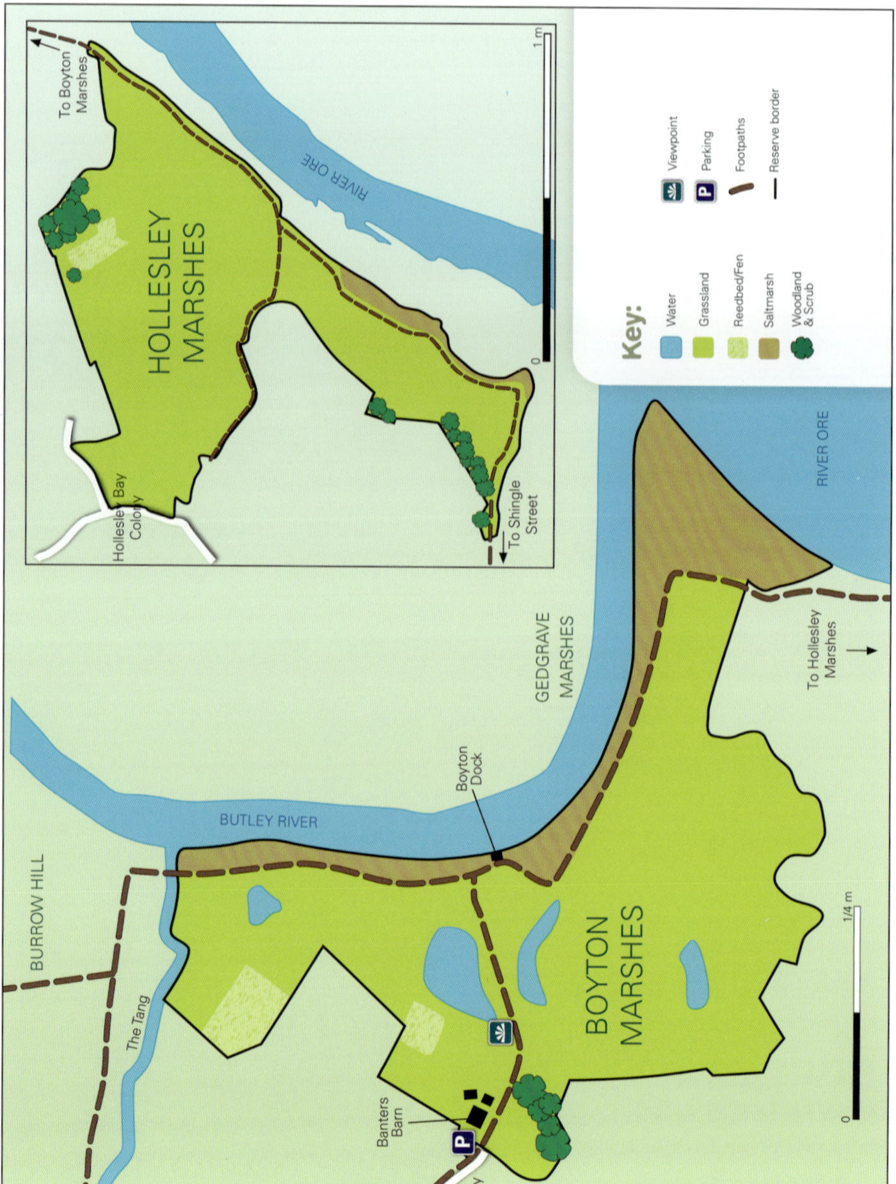

PEACEFUL PLACE: Boyton Marshes offer tranquility and good birdwatching. Barn owl, inset, is one of the reserve's specialities.

Geography and history

The panorama of Butley Creek, with Boyton Marshes on its west bank, can be viewed best from the summit of Burrow Hill. From here the creek and grazing marshes are seen in the foreground and, stretching beyond them, the Alde/Ore estuary, Havergate Island, Orford Ness and finally the open sea. This hill was occupied by Anglo Saxons – graves and domestic ware have recently been discovered on the summit.

The landscape has changed over the centuries as farmers have built river walls and dykes to enclose, and then drain, the reedbeds and saltmarsh of the once-expansive estuary. The Dutch engineers who probably built these walls in the 17th Century used the traditional technique of excavating a dyke and using the 'borrowed' clay and mud to construct a parallel embankment on the seaward side. These 'borrow' dykes can be seen inside the river walls throughout the reserve.

From the Middle Ages to fairly recent times, Butley Creek was a busy waterway. Grain was ferried upstream to Butley Mills and sailing barges would call at Boyton Dock, now a familiar landmark below the river wall.

The dock was used from 1639 for the export of valuable white clay from a deposit on a neighbouring farm. This was taken to London, Holland and North America to be used in the manufacture of Delftware pottery. Some of the profits from this were used by the Warner family to support the Mary Warner Almshouses in the nearby village of Boyton.

The dock was also used to receive coal from the north of England, to export straw to London for carriage horses and to bring in return a cargo of manure for the fields.

By the 19th Century, the boats would have been Thames barges, a few of which are still used as pleasure boats on the local estuaries. Coprolite mineral deposits, rich in phosphate and used in the making of fertiliser, were dug locally and exported from the dock until 1857. The trade was then resurrected and continued to the late 1880s.

During the Second World War, the fields were used as a tank training ground. Concrete blockhouses still on the marshes are reminders of this austere time. Life-size models of tanks were pulled from one blockhouse to another while being shot at by real tanks, giving the tank teams good target practice.

Concrete foundations for the Nissen huts, in which the tanks and ammunition were stored and the models were made, can be seen at Banter's Barn near the reserve car park. Two of the Nissen huts remain. After the war, this was a quiet, forgotten corner. It was one of the few remaining lowland wet grassland sites in the area, frequented by walkers, fisherman and sailors.

The RSPB purchased the 57-hectare (ha) reserve in 1990 and aims to maintain this remote tranquillity but also to improve the environment for birds and other wildlife. Since its purchase the reserve has been under the particular care of Honorary Warden Reg Etheridge. Help is given by a group of volunteers from the RSPB Woodbridge Local Group.

The grazing marshes have been returned to traditional management – and the birds have flourished.

This is a working reserve, so there are no hides or facilities except a small car park. The reserve can be explored by means of public footpaths. The surviving farm building, Banter's Barn at the reserve entrance, has been restored but several original timber-framed byres with pantile roofs have had to be demolished as the timbers were unsafe.

Beyond the barn, a copse of mixed trees and shrubs has been planted – Coates' Copse. It acknowledges the contribution of Colin and Shirley Coates to the work of the RSPB Woodbridge Local Group.

ECHOES OF WARTIME: Reminders of the Second World War can still be seen on the marshes.

BIRD'S EYE VIEW: Boyton Marshes looking north with Butley River in the background.

KEY TO SUCCESS: Grazing by pedigree Hereford cattle is an important part of the reserve's management.

Habitats and management

Boyton Marshes are part of the Suffolk Coast & Heaths Area of Outstanding Natural Beauty. Many of the developments on the site have been funded through Higher Level Stewardship and Environmentally Sensitive Area agreements – both sources of Government funding.

The reserve consists of grazing marshes, with an extensive network of drainage ditches, many of which contain patches of reedbed. Farmland rises gently to the west and the reserve is bordered to the east by the borrow dyke, the river wall, saltmarshes and the Butley River. Its northern boundary is the River Tang and to the south it extends to the Alde/Ore estuary opposite Havergate Island.

Since 1990, the reserve's numbers of breeding and wintering birds have expanded year by year. Almost 200 bird species have now been recorded on the reserve, with more than 50 breeding regularly.

The key to this success has been grazing by cattle and water-level management, combined with lowering the ground level to create a scrape – the Boyton Flash. Several islands have been created in the scrape to provide breeding sites for avocets.

Drainage water and water from natural springs on the adjacent farmland drains into the system of ditches across the reserve's water meadows which lead into the reed-lined borrow dykes and then, via the Tang River sluice, into the estuary. At several points the water flow in the ditches is controlled by bunds, or earth banks, with connecting pipes whose upper ends are adjusted to the desired water level on each side.

During the winter, water levels are raised to fill the scrape and create lagoons in several of the fields where wildfowl and waders can roost and feed on vegetation or on worms and other soil invertebrates.

From May to October, the water levels are lowered and the short grass, needed to attract ground-nesting redshanks and lapwings, is maintained by a herd of about 100 Hereford cattle that graze the meadows in rotation. Low densities are kept until the chicks fledge in early June. Thereafter the stocking levels are increased, moving into fields as the ground-nesting birds complete their breeding. The rough, grassy sward is also grazed by Canada and greylag geese.

Some fields are cut for hay and any remaining rushes or thistles and nettles are mown in early autumn. The ditches are cleared one side at a time in rotation to maintain the water flow and drainage.

The saltmarshes and areas of estuarine mud are equally important feeding grounds for waders and wildfowl. Here, ducks such as teals and wigeons feed at low tide on seeds and insects in the saltmarsh vegetation and waders use their long beaks to probe the mud for invertebrates such as Hydrobia snails, Corophium shrimps, and ragworms.

UNOBTRUSIVE: Water voles are present on the reserve but are only seen infrequently. A recent addition to the site's wildlife is the willow emerald damselfly, below, which has spread into Suffolk from the Continent.

Fauna

Most of the small mammals on the reserve, short-tailed field voles, water voles and wood mice, are well hidden from humans but are hunted for food by barn owls and kestrels. Stoats and weasels can easily be seen by the quiet observer as they scurry across the footpaths.

Foxes, stalking along the hedgerows, are a common sight in the early morning and the occasional otter, badger and various deer may visit the reserve. There are rabbits around in the drier areas, providing food for the foxes. In spring hares attract our attention on the grazing marshes with their boxing displays.

Common, and occasionally grey, seals venture into the river and may stay for several weeks, lying on the mud or simply popping their heads out of the water, revealing their large round eyes.

In the borrow dykes and smaller ditches, frogs and toads deposit their spawn while eels and rudd, once caught by the local boys, now provide a good food supply for herons and cormorants.

The dykes also provide places for dragonflies and damselflies to deposit their eggs on the underwater plants. From June to August the adults emerge from the water to range and feed over wide territories. Southern hawkers, common darters and four-spotted chasers may be joined by migrant hawker dragonflies, together with common blue, azure and large red damselflies. Willow emerald damselflies, a recent arrival on the Suffolk coast, have been seen at Boyton since 2010.

On May evenings, clouds of delicate ephemeral mayflies fly over the water surface trailing their paired 'tails' before mating and laying their eggs in the water.

Along the river wall small tortoiseshell, meadow brown and gatekeeper butterflies can be seen flying on fine warm days. Migrant painted ladies may rest on the ground when conditions are favourable and peacock and red admiral butterflies can usually be seen feeding on the nectar of the bramble flowers.

Wasp spiders, with their striped abdomens, may be seen guarding their webs in the grass and ground lackey moths flutter low over the saltmarsh plants.

Flora

The range of flora on the reserve reflects the distinct habitats here. In the saltmarsh, characteristic plants such as marsh samphire or glasswort, known also as poor man's asparagus, grow on the muddy margins and the pink thrift of early summer, flowers on the drier parts.

In July and August the purple sea lavender and sea aster create a striking border to the muddy foreshore. On the river wall, clumps of shiny, spinach-like leaves of sea beet and the aromatic sea wormwood grow among the sea couch grass.

The water-loving plants of the ditches flourish in the fresh water that moves steadily through to the borrow dykes. Many are reed-fringed and among the reeds forget-me-nots, water mint, yellow iris, figwort, purple loosestrife and the deadly hemlock flower through the summer season. Beneath the water surface, water crowfoot leaves move in the slow current, the small white flowers projecting above the water.

Plants of light, sandy soils are often very localised. On the dry margins of the track down to the reserve the tiny white flowers of spring beauty, introduced from North America, cover the ground in spring. Beside the track leading to the river wall, dittander, an unusual coastal plant, can be seen. It has dense clusters of white flowers on robust stems.

Main photo: REG ETHERIDGE, inset: ANDY HAY (rspb-images.com)

SALTMARSH: Large numbers of waders use this area of the reserve, and, inset, sea lavender creates a striking border to the foreshore.

Boyton & Hollesley Marshes

Wildlife season by season

WINTER: DECEMBER, JANUARY, FEBRUARY

A walk along the sea wall in winter is a memorable experience. Up to 2,000 wigeons and 600 teals may be feeding in compact flocks in the flooded areas of the grazing marshes. When disturbed they fly and wheel around, the wigeon's distinctive whistling call and whirring wings being characteristic sounds of winter.

In the wet meadows to the south of the reserve wigeons feed among the larger wintering wildfowl. Up to 200 greylag and 800 Canada geese and a few mute swans regularly feed here. Occasionally they are joined by other goose species, such as tundra bean, brent, barnacle and white-front.

Curlews, lapwings and a few common snipe can be seen on the reserve through most of the year, but are here in much larger numbers in winter, with an occasional jack snipe joining them. Throughout the autumn and winter this part of the reserve provides perfect feeding conditions for flocks of fieldfares, redwings and starlings.

Resident gadwalls and tufted ducks can be seen alongside mallards, coots and moorhens on the borrow dyke. Looking towards the river by the dock, stonechats, meadow and rock pipits, with occasional flocks of twites, can be seen as they feed on seeds, insects and the numerous spiders among the saltmarsh plants.

The distinct white of little egrets stands out as they feed in the saltmarsh lagoons or fly out across the river, their yellow feet trailing behind them.

Also from the dock, as high tide approaches, flocks of avocets are seen flying up the estuary and returning as the ebb begins. On the mud, among the herring gulls and black-headed gulls, redshanks feed along the tide margins, occasionally taking flight and emitting their distinctive call.

Photo: CHRIS GOMERSHALL (rspb-images.com)

DISTINCTIVE CALLS: The whistling of wigeons is a familiar winter sound at Boyton Marshes.

Main photo: CHRIS GOMERSHALL (rspb-images.com), inset, JON EVANS

WADER HAVEN: Redshanks, main photo, and black-tailed godwits, inset, are two species of wader that can often be seen around the marshes.

Flocks of dunlins may appear, flickering dark and white before they also settle to feed. Ringed plovers move busily along the water's edge as small groups of knots rest on the mud and the black-tailed godwits probe under the water with their long bills.

On the water, little grebes, often with visiting goldeneyes and great crested grebes, dive and resurface as they feed. Very occasionally a red-throated diver may also be seen.

Barn owls are well known to those who visit and work on the reserve. The sight of their pale shapes, with wings flapping and gliding as they quarter the reeds on a winter day at dusk, never fails to excite.

This part of rural Suffolk is an important area for barn owls. There are at least ten pairs in the neighbourhood, often using the nestboxes erected as part of the Suffolk Community Barn Owl Project. They like the dry climate and there are plenty of small mammals in the rough grasslands and reedbeds for easy hunting.

Marsh harriers do not nest on the reserve but regularly hunt over the reedbeds and pastures. Common buzzards, and occasionally a rough-legged buzzard, may also be seen. Indeed, common buzzards have recently established a foothold in this part of coastal Suffolk – the woodland and heathland of the Sandlings providing suitable territory for feeding and nesting.

Boyton Marshes is a regular winter haunt of peregrine falcons. They fly powerfully to soar and stoop over the river, often capturing a wader in flight. The smaller merlin visits the reserve, often hunting pipits over the saltmarsh, while hen harriers may also be observed.

SPRING: MARCH, APRIIL, MAY

The first sign of spring is often groups of wintering redwings, fieldfares and starlings, gathering on the grazing marshes before their departure over the North Sea. Oystercatchers, which choose neighbouring estuaries for their winter feeding, return to the salt marshes by early March. The wildfowl will also be decreasing in numbers as they leave for their breeding grounds to the north.

This is also the time when the first summer migrants appear. Perhaps a wheatear may bound ahead of the walker on the river wall or a party of sand martins may dash overhead.

Breeding water rails may emit their shrill screams from the depths of the reeds. Stock doves take advantage of the owl-windows on the gable ends of Banter's Barn to gain access to the building in which they construct their nests.

By April, many passage migrants are visiting the reserve, pausing to feed and rest on the flooded fields or on the saltmarsh and mud beyond the river wall. Passage waders encountered at this time may include greenshanks, ringed plovers, spotted redshanks, whimbrels and green, common and occasionally wood sandpipers.

Chiffchaffs are usually the first of the breeding songbirds to be heard among the trees, followed by blackcaps and garden warblers, with Cetti's and sedge warblers, and common and lesser whitethroats in the scrubby brambles and hawthorns.

This is one of the few places on the Suffolk coast where yellow wagtails still breed in the grasslands. Reed warblers are nest-building in the reeds, wary of the parasitic cuckoos searching for nests in which to lay their eggs. Resident reed buntings nest in the scrub and reeds and pied wagtails build their nests in the farm buildings.

Swallows return to feed over the insect-rich meadows and the wartime blockhouses provide the perfect nesting sites for them. Sand martins and house martins feed constantly over the reserve, joined in early May by swifts. While keeping your eyes to the skies, look out for passage red kites, honey buzzards and ospreys.

It is very satisfying for the wardens and volunteer helpers to know that breeding lapwings have increased year by year, so

Main photo: ANDY HAY (rspb-images.com); inset, CHRIS GOMERSHALL (rspb-images.com)

FOOTHOLDS ESTABLISHED: Main photo, common buzzard is a species which has become a local breeder. Yellow wagtail, inset, has declined but still breeds on the reserve.

that there are now about twenty breeding pairs. This makes Boyton Marshes the best lapwing breeding site on the Suffolk coast. Redshanks are also nesting here and skylarks breed in the drier fields.

Such success is due to careful management of the grazing meadows to give areas of smooth, short grass for lapwings – which prefer to have unbroken views from their nests – and tussocks and clumps of rushes to provide the slightly raised and protected nest sites preferred by redshanks. These ground-nesting birds have most to fear from gulls and carrion crows which feed on their eggs and young.

TAKING A REST: A common darter alights on a fence – the species is one of the reserve's many dragonflies.

The construction of islands in the scrape and the growth of the reeds and other vegetation along the margins have created breeding sites for water-birds. The most striking of these are the avocets which have spread here from Havergate Island. The islands in the scrape have created space for up to a dozen or more pairs to breed.

As you watch these fabulous birds from the reserve path, performing their courtship rituals and defending their shallow nests and their young, you can see them co-operating with the black-headed gulls also nesting there. Together they drive away the predatory herring gulls and lesser black-backed gulls which cause such trouble elsewhere. The result has been most pleasing numbers of fully fledged chicks.

Other breeding birds include several pairs of gadwall and tufted duck as well as the more numerous mallards, moorhens and little grebes.

SUMMER: June, July, August

Through the early summer the barn owls hunt to feed their young on the plentiful small mammals. Sparrowhawks are often seen as they fly fast along the hedgerows and the characteristic silhouette of a little owl, a species that also nests in the reserve, may be observed on one of the fence posts.

From the river wall, little, Sandwich and common terns can be seen patrolling the shallower waters and then hovering and plunging to emerge with a small fish. Dashing hobbies are seen hawking dragonflies over the grazing meadows and a flash of bright colour or a shrill whistle reveals a kingfisher in flight between the reeds.

Common blue, azure and large red damselflies fly over the water of the dykes and the bright purple of flowering sea lavender and sea aster adds life to the saltmarsh. Peacock and red admiral butterflies gather nectar in the hedgerows.

Most of the songbirds are silent and by August the screaming swifts and their young are on the point of departure. Returning migrants begin to arrive – first greenshanks, followed by wood, green and common sandpipers, whimbrels and then larger groups of curlews and black-tailed godwits. Their length of stay depends on the water levels, as the earthworms and other soil invertebrates will be nearer the surface when the soil is damp.

AUTUMN: SEPTEMBER, OCTOBER, NOVEMBER

Autumn begins slowly on the Suffolk coast. Even if the weather is still fine and dry the numbers of waders feeding on the reserve increases steadily. The birds are able to move to the grazing meadows as the tide rises to cover the mud and then return to the estuary as the tides ebbs.

Passerine migrants such as whinchat and wheatear may be present in the areas of scrub and hedgerow, particularly when the wind blows in from the east. During one such period, Suffolk's first isabelline shrike was found near Banter's Barn. Recently four glossy ibis spent several weeks feeding around the scrape and lagoons. Another recent rare vagrant was a single sandhill crane.

By the end of the autumn remarkably large numbers of birds are feeding on the estuary or on the grazing marshes. About 200 curlews, up to 300 redshanks, 200 lapwings, substantial numbers of avocets, black-tailed godwits and a few knots and ringed plovers are likely to be seen. The occasional pintail or shoveler may be picked out among the large numbers of wigeons and teals arriving for the winter on the grazing marshes.

Photo: JENNY JAMES

Photos: JON EVANS

MARVELS OF MIGRATION: Wheatear, left, and whinchat, inset, are regular passage visitors, but glossy ibis, above, is a rare vagrant.

INCREDIBLE JOURNEY: This sandhill crane's historic passage into Suffolk's ornithological history represents one of the most amazing avian events ever recorded in the county. Thought probably to be of the species' northern race which inhabits the Great Lakes area of North America, overwintering mainly in central Florida, it was probably 'kidnapped' by Hurricane Katia in 2011. First seen in Britain over Dunbar, Lothian, on September 16, it was tracked down the coast of Scotland and England, arriving at Barnby, Suffolk, on October 2. During the course of that day it flew down the Suffolk coast, arriving at North Warren around noon. During the afternoon it was seen over Havergate Island before touching down at Boyton Marshes reserve and staying in the Boyton/Hollesley Marshes area until October 7. A total of about 4,000 birdwatchers were lured to the area to see this celebrated visitor.

The story did not end here, however, as the bird wintered with common cranes near Badajoz in Extremadura, Spain.

GHOSTLY PRESENCE: Barn owls are a familiar sight at Boyton and Hollesley Marshes.

Main photo: JON EVANS. Inset, JOHN BRIDGES (rspb-images.com)

RESERVE INFORMATION – Boyton Marshes

Opening times

Access at all times on public footpaths only.

How to get there

From the A12 at Woodbridge take the A1152 and then the B1084 to Butley. Turn right at the Oyster Inn, follow the lane and turn left by the St Andrew sculpture on the farm wall at the Capel St Andrew crossroads. At the first right-angle bend follow the road to the right, at the second go straight on down a farm track towards the estuary. The car park is 300m down the concrete road just before the barn.

Further information

Contact: The Havergate Warden, email: havergate.island@rspb.org.uk or see www.rspb.org.uk/boytonmarshes

Hollesley Marshes

EASY WALKING: Hollesley Marshes is an ideal site for a bracing stroll and the main path from Shingle Street takes the visitor alongside Alde/Ore estuary where evidence of old river wall defences can be seen, inset.

A short distance downstream along the Alde/Ore estuary from Boyton Marshes you will find another RSPB reserve. Looking down from the river wall which, like those at Boyton, was probably first built in the 17th Century to reclaim the land from saltmarsh, you can see traditional water meadows with a herd of Jersey dairy cows, rows of hybrid black poplars and reed-lined ditches.

In the 20th Century Grove Farm, on Hollesley Marshes, was run for many years by HM Prisons and, in the days when there was a borstal here, the boys were trained to work on the land.

They worked with the prison's famous Suffolk Punch horses – now owned by the independent Suffolk Punch Trust – and learned the skills needed for farm work, including dairy farming. The dairy buildings can still be seen on the edge of the marshes, below the prison on the rising ground.

The land had been neglected for some years before the RSPB acquired it in 2006. The drains were blocked and the fields were waterlogged. It was decided to create a reserve where the land is used to show that wildlife can co-exist with farming, provided that traditional methods are used.

This is a classic water meadow and is now used by a local farmer for cattle pasture and hay-making, re-instating a regime used over the centuries in many parts of Britain and which creates ideal conditions for wildlife. The water levels are being controlled, with foot drains and sluices and a shallow permanent scrape with islands, to create another wildlife haven.

Each season has its own charm but perhaps the richest season is winter. Marsh harriers, a major attraction of the Suffolk coast, often visit to hunt, as do common buzzards which are recent colonists.

Boyton & Hollesley Marshes

Looking across the scrape and grazing meadows on a sunny winter day, the bright colours of the male wigeons and the green flash of the teals will catch your attention as good numbers of both species feed alongside resident mallards, mute swans and greylag and Canada geese. They are joined from time to time by increasingly large groups of brent geese.

A grey heron or a little egret may flap lazily across the meadows where flocks of curlews and black-tailed godwits may feed almost unseen, only to rise up when disturbed, showing their dramatic markings. A common snipe may zig-zag away below them or a fox may be hunting along the hedgerows.

There is plenty of cover and food for wintering passerines. Meadow pipits feed on the saltmarsh, stonechats can regularly be seen in the brambles and substantial flocks of goldfinches move between the patches of thistledown in the water meadows. Migrant fieldfares, redwings and starlings all feed in the rough grass.

From the river wall, flocks of dunlins, redshanks and occasional oystercatchers can be seen feeding on the mud. Across the river on the southernmost point of Orford Ness, a group of cormorants stand like sentinels guarding the river entrance. The haunting calls from groups of avocets may be heard as they fly up or down the estuary or land to feed in the scrape.

In spring and summer, Hollesley Marshes is at its most appealing and increasing numbers of species are breeding here. Water plants, such as common reed, sedges, bur-reeds, and rushes line the network of ditches. In spring, the small blue flowers of brooklime and the striking yellow of marsh marigold are followed through the summer by water mint, pink water speedwell, bur-marigold, water plantain and water parsnip.

On the saltmarsh, the inconspicuous plants and flowers of sea purslane, sea wormwood and sea plantain provide a background for progressive splashes of colour as the

WINTER FEEDING: Dark-bellied brent geese find the reserve's grasslands and the estuary to their liking.

season advances. The bright pink thrift of early summer is followed by the blues and purples of sea aster and sea lavender.

The water-filled ditches are home to breeding moorhens and mallards and to the aquatic larvae of dragonflies and damselflies, from which the adults hatch progressively through the summer. The occasional otter may be seen emerging from the undergrowth as swallows, swifts and sand martins chase insects overhead.

The islands on the scrape attract several pairs of avocets each year. Their breeding success is limited, but should improve as the scrape becomes more established. The wardens are working hard to create conditions to attract breeding waders and in time lapwings and redshanks should be lured in to take advantage of a prime breeding site.

However, the reedbeds, hedgerows, clumps of trees, the old osier bed and ditches provide secluded and secure breeding sites for treecreepers and the many resident blackbirds, thrushes and tits. Migrant sedge and garden warblers, chiffchaffs, blackcaps and an occasional willow warbler also make their nests here. The call of the male cuckoo can be frequently heard in spring and the females take advantage of the numerous reed warbler nests to lay their eggs.

Cetti's warblers nest low in the tree-lined ditches attracting your attention with their abrupt and explosive song. Reed buntings flit across the reedbeds in search of food for their young and linnets, together with common and lesser whitethroats, nest in the bushes and brambles. From the trees in the osier bed, turtle doves call as they prepare to mate and breed and green and great spotted woodpeckers excavate the rotting wood for food.

In this quiet corner, kestrels choose the poplar trees to nest and a pair of barn owls has discovered a hidden retreat in which to raise a family.

With its position on the coast, Hollesley Marshes provides a haven for passage migrants in spring and autumn. Migrant wader species such as greenshank, green and common sandpiper, take advantage of the shelter and feeding sites to rest on their journeys between summer and winter quarters. From the river wall, the haunting call of a group of whimbrels might attract our attention as they fly past. Migrant knots and dunlins can be seen feeding on the muddy foreshore and where there are bushes or brambles, wheatears, redstarts and whinchats can be seen resting as they pass through.

Beyond the scrape, on the far side of the reserve, the old osier bed is such a favoured resting place for migrants that it is a regular ringing station. Many interesting species have been caught here, including rare migrants such as bluethroats and a red-flanked bluetail.

The process of renewal of a precious and tranquil fragment of traditional landscape is well under way at Hollesley Marshes. It is most rewarding for wardens and visitors alike to see the way that the wildlife is developing and flourishing.

SUNNY DISPOSITION: Marsh marigolds bring a splash of colour to the reserve's water margins.

MARSHLAND EXPANSE: The wide open spaces of the Hollesley reserve are crossed by ditches and dykes.

Photo: JENNY JAMES

Reserve reflections: special memories of Boyton Marshes

Looking back at Boyton

'Boyton Marshes were part of Dock Farm up to the 1930s and my grandfather worked on the farm for Mr Minter. He would recall how, in the early years of the century, the dock was busy with shipping. In the days before the local roads were properly surfaced this was the common means of transportation. Grain and cattle were shipped off the dock and coal, seeds and general provisions were brought in.

By the time that I, as a young girl in the 1930s, walked the marshes the dock was no longer used for commercial trade. I lived in Butley at the time and we thought nothing of walking to Boyton Marshes and back to collect samphire which we would pickle in vinegar and use as a salad with cold meat. In autumn the fields were dotted with mushrooms and we would collect basketfuls and take them home to fry.

During the war I moved away to Hertfordshire, in service, and when I came back to visit relatives I found that I could not get down to the marshes as they had been taken over by the Army. You can still see some of their buildings and gun and searchlight emplacements.

Seven years ago I returned to my roots. I live in the Mary Warner Almshouses in the village and I love walking the marshes. On the dock I have put a seat which is for the use of anyone who, like me, just enjoys resting and watching the birds in this beautiful and tranquil place.'

Mrs Mary Chittock, née Foreman

RESERVE INFORMATION - Hollesley Marshes

Opening times

Access at all times from public footpaths only.

How to get there

Leave the A12 at Woodbridge and follow the minor roads through Hollesley, past Duck Corner and Dum-boy Cottage to Shingle Street.
From the Shingle Street parking area, retrace your route across the bridge over the tidal creek.
Take the path to the right along the river wall on the inland side of the creek to find an information board in a short distance.
For a longer walk approach along the river wall from Boyton Marshes.

Further information

Contact: The Havergate Warden, email: havergate.island@rspb.org.uk

Boyton & Hollesley Marshes

Tick 'em off

A checklist of Suffolk birds

This table enables observers to keep a 'ticklist' of species they have seen on the six reserves featured in this book. This is the official list, but not order, of species recorded in Suffolk, as at April 2012. Some species names are those used by the British Ornithologists' Union and in some cases differ from those used in the text of this book, which adopts a more colloquial approach.

	DINGLE MARSHES & DUNWICH FOREST	MINSMERE	NORTH WARREN & ALDRINGHAM WALKS	SNAPE RESERVE	HAVERGATE ISLAND	BOYTON & HOLLESLEY MARSHES
DIVERS						
RED-THROATED DIVER						
BLACK-THROATED DIVER						
GREAT NORTHERN DIVER						
YELLOW (WHITE)-BILLED DIVER						
GREBES						
LITTLE GREBE						
GREAT CRESTED GREBE						
RED-NECKED GREBE						
SLAVONIAN GREBE						
BLACK-NECKED GREBE						
TUBENOSES						
NORTHERN FULMAR						
CORY'S SHEARWATER						
GREAT SHEARWATER						
SOOTY SHEARWATER						
MANX SHEARWATER						
BALEARIC SHEARWATER						
LEACH'S STORM PETREL						
EUROPEAN STORM PETREL						
GANNETS						
NORTHERN GANNET						
CORMORANTS						
GREAT CORMORANT						
EUROPEAN SHAG						
HERONS						
GREAT BITTERN						
LITTLE BITTERN						
BLACK-CROWNED NIGHT HERON						
SQUACCO HERON						
CATTLE EGRET						
LITTLE EGRET						
GREAT (WHITE) EGRET						
GREY HERON						
PURPLE HERON						
BLACK STORK						
WHITE STORK						
GLOSSY IBIS						
EURASIAN SPOONBILL						
SWANS						
MUTE SWAN						
TUNDRA (BEWICK'S) SWAN						
WHOOPER SWAN						

GEESE

BEAN GOOSE (TUNDRA & TAIGA)
PINK-FOOTED GOOSE
GREATER WHITE-FRONTED GOOSE
GREYLAG GOOSE
SNOW GOOSE
CANADA GOOSE
BARNACLE GOOSE
BRENT GOOSE, inc. PALE BELLIED & BLACK BRANT
EGYPTIAN GOOSE
RED-BREASTED GOOSE

DUCKS

RUDDY SHELDUCK
COMMON SHELDUCK
MANDARIN DUCK
EURASIAN WIGEON
AMERICAN WIGEON
GADWALL
COMMON TEAL
GREEN-WINGED TEAL
MALLARD
NORTHERN PINTAIL
GARGANEY
BLUE-WINGED TEAL
BAIKAL TEAL
NORTHERN SHOVELER
RED-CRESTED POCHARD
COMMON POCHARD
RING-NECKED DUCK
FERRUGINOUS DUCK
TUFTED DUCK
GREATER SCAUP
LESSER SCAUP
COMMON EIDER
KING EIDER
LONG-TAILED DUCK
COMMON SCOTER
VELVET SCOTER
BUFFLEHEAD
COMMON GOLDENEYE
SMEW
RED-BREASTED MERGANSER
GOOSANDER
RUDDY DUCK

BIRDS OF PREY

EUROPEAN HONEY BUZZARD
BLACK KITE
RED KITE
WHITE-TAILED EAGLE
EURASIAN MARSH HARRIER
HEN HARRIER
MONTAGU'S HARRIER
PALLID HARRIER
NORTHERN GOSHAWK
EURASIAN SPARROWHAWK
COMMON BUZZARD
ROUGH-LEGGED BUZZARD
GREATER SPOTTED EAGLE
OSPREY
COMMON KESTREL
LESSER KESTREL

RED-FOOTED FALCON
MERLIN
EURASIAN HOBBY
ELEONORA'S FALCON
GYR FALCON
PEREGRINE FALCON

QUAILS, PARTRIDGES & PHEASANTS

GREY PARTRIDGE
RED-LEGGED PARTRIDGE
COMMON PHEASANT
GOLDEN PHEASANT
COMMON QUAIL

CRAKES & RAILS

WATER RAIL
SPOTTED CRAKE
LITTLE CRAKE
BAILLON'S CRAKE
CORNCRAKE
COMMON MOORHEN
COMMON COOT
ALLEN'S GALLINULE

CRANES

COMMON CRANE
SANDHILL CRANE

BUSTARDS

LITTLE BUSTARD
MACQUEEN'S (HOUBARA) BUSTARD
GREAT BUSTARD

WADERS

EURASIAN OYSTERCATCHER
BLACK-WINGED STILT
PIED AVOCET
STONE CURLEW
CREAM-COLOURED COURSER
COLLARED PRATICOLE
ORIENTAL PRATINCOLE
BLACK-WINGED PRATINCOLE
LITTLE (RINGED) PLOVER
RINGED PLOVER
KENTISH PLOVER
GREATER SAND PLOVER
EURASIAN DOTTEREL
EUROPEAN GOLDEN PLOVER
PACIFIC GOLDEN PLOVER
AMERICAN GOLDEN PLOVER
GREY PLOVER
SOCIABLE PLOVER (SOCIABLE LAPWING)
NORTHERN LAPWING
RED KNOT
SANDERLING
SEMIPALMATED SANDPIPER
LITTLE STINT
TEMMINCK'S STINT
WHITE-RUMPED SANDPIPER
BAIRD'S SANDPIPER
PECTORAL SANDPIPER
CURLEW SANDPIPER
PURPLE SANDPIPER
DUNLIN
BROAD-BILLED SANDPIPER
STILT SANDPIPER

BUFF-BREASTED SANDPIPER
RUFF
JACK SNIPE
COMMON SNIPE
GREAT SNIPE
LONG-BILLED DOWITCHER
EURASIAN WOODCOCK
BLACK-TAILED GODWIT
BAR-TAILED GODWIT
WHIMBREL
EURASIAN CURLEW
SPOTTED REDSHANK
COMMON REDSHANK
MARSH SANDPIPER
COMMON GREENSHANK
GREATER YELLOWLEGS
LESSER YELLOWLEGS
GREEN SANDPIPER
WOOD SANDPIPER
TEREK SANDPIPER
COMMON SANDPIPER
SPOTTED SANDPIPER
RUDDY TURNSTONE
WILSON'S PHALAROPE
RED-NECKED PHALAROPE
GREY PHALAROPE

SKUAS

POMARINE SKUA
ARCTIC SKUA
LONG-TAILED SKUA
GREAT SKUA

GULLS

BLACK-HEADED GULL
SLENDER-BILLED GULL
COMMON GULL
RING-BILLED GULL
MEDITERRANEAN GULL
HERRING GULL
YELLOW-LEGGED GULL
AUDOUIN'S GULL
CASPIAN GULL
GREAT BLACK-BACKED GULL
LESSER BLACK-BACKED GULL
ROSS'S GULL
LITTLE GULL
KITTIWAKE
SABINE'S GULL
GLAUCOUS GULL
ICELAND GULL
IVORY GULL
LAUGHING GULL
FRANKLIN'S GULL

TERNS

GULL-BILLED TERN
CASPIAN TERN
LESSER CRESTED TERN
SANDWICH TERN
ROSEATE TERN
COMMON TERN
ARCTIC TERN
SOOTY TERN

LITTLE TERN
WHISKERED TERN
BLACK TERN
WHITE-WINGED BLACK TERN

AUKS

COMMON GUILLEMOT
RAZORBILL
BLACK GUILLEMOT
LITTLE AUK
ATLANTIC PUFFIN

SANDGROUSE

PALLAS'S SANDGROUSE

DOVES & PIGEONS

FERAL PIGEON
STOCK DOVE
COMMON WOOD PIGEON
EURASIAN COLLARED DOVE
EUROPEAN TURTLE DOVE
ORIENTAL TURTLE DOVE

PARAKEETS

ROSE-RINGED PARAKEET

CUCKOOS

COMMON CUCKOO
YELLOW-BILLED CUCKOO
GREAT SPOTTED CUCKOO

OWLS

BARN OWL
LITTLE OWL
SCOPS OWL
SNOWY OWL
TAWNY OWL
LONG-EARED OWL
SHORT-EARED OWL
TENGMALM'S OWL

NIGHTJARS

NIGHTJAR

SWIFTS

SWIFT
PALLID SWIFT
ALPINE SWIFT

KINGFISHERS

COMMON KINGFISHER

BEE EATERS & THEIR ALLIES

EUROPEAN BEEEATER
EUROPEAN ROLLER
HOOPOE

WOODPECKERS

EURASIAN WRYNECK
GREEN WOODPECKER
GREAT SPOTTED WOODPECKER
LESSER SPOTTED WOODPECKER

LARKS

GREATER SHORT-TOED LARK
WOODLARK
SKYLARK
CRESTED LARK
SHORE LARK

SWALLOWS & MARTINS

SAND MARTIN
BARN SWALLOW
RED-RUMPED SWALLOW

HOUSE MARTIN

PIPITS

RICHARD'S PIPIT
BLYTH'S PIPIT
TAWNY PIPIT
OLIVE-BACKED PIPIT
TREE PIPIT
MEADOW PIPIT
RED-THROATED PIPIT
ROCK PIPIT
WATER PIPIT

WAGTAILS

YELLOW WAGTAIL, inc. BLUE, GREY-HEADED
CITRINE WAGTAIL
GREY WAGTAIL
PIED WAGTAIL, INCL WHITE WAGTAIL

WAXWINGS

BOHEMIAN WAXWING

DIPPERS

DIPPER, inc BLACK-BELLIED

WRENS

WREN

ACCENTORS

HEDGE ACCENTOR (DUNNOCK)
ALPINE ACCENTOR

ROBINS

EUROPEAN ROBIN

NIGHTINGALES & THEIR ALLIES

THRUSH NIGHTINGALE
COMMON NIGHTINGALE
BLUETHROAT
RED-FLANKED BLUETAIL
SIBERIAN BLUE ROBIN

REDSTARTS

BLACK REDSTART
COMMON REDSTART

CHATS

WHINCHAT
STONECHAT
SIBERIAN STONECHAT

WHEATEARS

NORTHERN WHEATEAR
ISABELLINE WHEATEAR
PIED WHEATEAR
DESERT WHEATEAR
WHITE-TAILED (WHITE-CROWNED BLACK) WHEATEAR

THRUSHES

WHITE'S THRUSH
RING OUZEL
COMMON BLACKBIRD
FIELDFARE
SONG THRUSH
REDWING
MISTLE THRUSH

WARBLERS

CETTI'S WARBLER
LANCEOLATED WARBLER
COMMON GRASSHOPPER WARBLER
RIVER WARBLER
SAVI'S WARBLER
AQUATIC WARBLER

SEDGE WARBLER
PADDYFIELD WARBLER
BLYTH'S REED WARBLER
MARSH WARBLER
EURASIAN REED WARBLER
GREAT REED WARBLER
EASTERN OLIVACEOUS WARBLER
BOOTED WARBLER
ICTERINE WARBLER
MELODIOUS WARBLER
DARTFORD WARBLER
MARMORAS WARBLER
SPECTACLED WARBLER
SUBALPINE WARBLER
BARRED WARBLER
SARDINIAN WARBLER
LESSER WHITETHROAT
COMMON WHITETHROAT
GARDEN WARBLER
BLACKCAP
GREENISH WARBLER
ARCTIC WARBLER
PALLAS' LEAF WARBLER
YELLOW-BROWED WARBLER
HUME'S (YELLOW-BROWED) WARBLER
RADDE'S WARBLER
DUSKY WARBLER
WESTERN BONELLI'S WARBLER
WOOD WARBLER
COMMON CHIFFCHAFF
WILLOW WARBLER

CRESTS

GOLDCREST
FIRECREST

FLYCATCHERS

SPOTTED FLYCATCHER
RED-BREASTED FLYCATCHER
COLLARED FLYCATCHER
PIED FLYCATCHER

BEARDED TIT (PARROTBILLS)

BEARDED TIT

TITS

LONG-TAILED TIT
MARSH TIT
WILLOW TIT
CRESTED TIT
COAL TIT
BLUE TIT
GREAT TIT

NUTHATCHES

WOOD NUTHATCH

TREECREEPERS

EURASIAN TREECREEPER
SHORT-TOED TREECREEPER

PENDULINE TITS

EURASIAN PENDULINE TIT

ORIOLES

EURASIAN GOLDEN ORIOLE

SHRIKES

ISABELLINE SHRIKE
RED-BACKED SHRIKE

LESSER GREY SHRIKE
GREAT (NORTHERN) GREY SHRIKE
SOUTHERN GREY SHRIKE
WOODCHAT SHRIKE

CORVIDS

EURASIAN JAY
BLACK-BILLED MAGPIE
SPOTTED NUTCRACKER
RED-BILLED CHOUGH
EURASIAN JACKDAW
ROOK
CARRION CROW
HOODED CROW
COMMON RAVEN

STARLINGS

COMMON STARLING
ROSY STARLING

SPARROWS

HOUSE SPARROW
EURASIAN TREE SPARROW

VIREOS

RED-EYED VIREO

FINCHES & CROSSBILLS

CHAFFINCH
BRAMBLING
EUROPEAN SERIN
EUROPEAN GREENFINCH
EUROPEAN GOLDFINCH
EURASIAN SISKIN
COMMON LINNET
TWITE
LESSER REDPOLL
COMMON REDPOLL ['MEALY' REDPOLL]
ARCTIC REDPOLL
TWO-BARRED CROSSBILL
COMMON CROSSBILL
PARROT CROSSBILL
TRUMPETER FINCH
COMMON (SCARLET) ROSEFINCH
COMMON BULLFINCH
HAWFINCH

AMERICAN SPARROWS

LARK SPARROW
WHITE-THROATED SPARROW

BUNTINGS

LAPLAND BUNTING
SNOW BUNTING
YELLOWHAMMER
PINE BUNTING
CIRL BUNTING
BLACK-HEADED BUNTING
YELLOW-BREASTED BUNTING
ORTOLAN BUNTING
RUSTIC BUNTING
LITTLE BUNTING
REED BUNTING
CORN BUNTING

Notes